ABOUT THE AUTHOR

Dr Al Waters has extensive experience in a wide range of roles in education and exam boards, including Head of Biology, an advisor for National Bodies and Trusts and a marker/moderator for AQA. As part of this he has marked the synoptic paper for both AQA and Edexcel. He is also the Founder and Chief Executive of Tranquillitas Ltd, a company that specialises in the use of modern media in education.

HOW THIS BOOK WAS WRITTEN

This book has evolved over a period of years. I am fortunate to have had a number of truly excellent students (Oxbridge and full UMS). Over the years I have ordered the transcript of all our school's A* papers and collated the essays. Where there were gaps I gave these students the past-paper essay titles and mark schemes and paid them to write 'model essays'. Then, as a trained marker, I edited them all to make sure they were written to an A* standard.

A colleague of mine, who has also marked for AQA, then went through them as a third independent determination of their grade. We have used this collection of essays in our school for a number of years with fantastic results. With the advent of the new specification, I have revisited them and made changes to reflect the new content.

Topics that are no longer at A-level have been removed and new content added, which has meant a number of particular large changes in the field of Ecology. This has been a surprisingly onerous undertaking, but I am very proud of the result. Someone then suggested to me that I should publish my work and this is the product – an analysis of over 40 titles and 25 A* essays.

TABLE OF CONTENTS

Table of Contents for Essays

Content	page

INTRODUCTION

The essay makes up the final question of paper 3 at A2. You must select one from a choice of two possible titles. It is worth 25 marks out of a possible 78. You would, therefore, expect to spend 40 to 45 minutes on it. In reality, you could have more time than this but many candidates rush to get to the essay and miss easy marks in the process. Marks in the essay are worth no more or less than any other in the paper. In my experience as a marker, students tend to find themselves in a band between 14 and 22 marks, with those essays at the upper end of this being around 3 to 4 sides long. This is equivalent to around two sides of typed A4. It is not really worth writing more than as it rarely adds more marks and you will sacrifice other marks in the paper. AQA's advice to teachers is that the marking and skills looked for in the new essays are the same as in the old. So the skills that worked before still hold true now.

How to approach the essay

The question requires you to select one essay title from a choice of two. My advice would be to look at both titles as soon as you open the paper. One of them will probably jump out as your favourite. Quickly start making your essay plan under that title. Turn back to the start of the paper and then, as ideas come to you, quickly add them to your plan, without breaking your 'flow' during the other questions. This means it will already have been turning over in your subconscious for over an hour by the time you start writing your essay. Further on in this introduction, I will discuss how the essay is marked and the aspects you will, therefore, need to consider when writing your plan. Remember, the point of the essay – in fact, all of your exams – is not to write a seminal work, but rather to get the highest possible number of marks. There are certain topics and styles of writing that are worth more marks than others. I am the first during term time to ask students to rise to the challenge, stretch themselves and maybe take a few risks at the same time; but exam week is about getting the highest grades you can. The exam board are reasonably transparent about what you need to do in order to achieve a top grade, so use this as an opportunity to give them what they want.

How to prepare for the essay

You've made a good start by buying the only specific preparation guide written by someone who knows what they are talking about! I have split the essays into three sections; Biochemistry and Cells, Ecology, and finally a catch-all section of others. This is ordered by the regularity with which they came up in the previous A-level. For instance, there is a Biochemistry based essay every two out of three years. There will be a bit of overlap, but it is a good place to start. It is surprising how little genetics and physiology essays come up, but I have looked at all the essay titles for the last 20 years and 75% fall into the first two categories.

In each section, the previous essay titles are grouped by similarity, such as those that have a stem of proteins. I have prepared a 'topics to consider' based on the mark schemes and then there follows an A* essay.

There is no need to do any specific revision, as the content will be the same as in any other part of the exam. A good place to begin would be to choose an essay title and do your revision without thinking about the essay. Then, as a method of revision, try to write an essay based on that title. This means you will be incorporating your essay writing into 'active revision' and killing two birds with one stone. I don't think it is possible to remember the 25 essays off by heart, but if you go into the exam knowing how to construct your essay, and what needs to be included, you will have done all that you can. I also have written some exemplar paragraphs that can be edited to fit a number of titles, which will be worth remembering. I would hope that your teacher has also set and marked 20 essays for you during the course of year 13. However, take any marks with a pinch of salt. Unlike with other marking, the essay is very subjective and so comes slowly with training and practice.

How the essay is marked
This is the only real difference between the old and new exam. However, AQA has run sessions for teachers showing that the same essays would get the same score under either criteria. This is explained below. Markers and examiners are using a 'best fit approach'. The markers who mark the essays tend to be a bit more experienced and have a 'feel' for a grade. There are no mark schemes as such, as there are in other papers, but rather these descriptors, which are taken from the AQA website.

(A*/A) 21 – 25 Marks

Extended beyond the specific content to include parts outside the specification.

The response shows a holistic approach to the question with a fully integrated answer that makes clear links between several different topics and the theme of the question.

The Biology is detailed with comprehensive A-level content. It uses appropriate terminology, and is both very well written and always clearly explained.

There are no significant errors or irrelevant material.

For top marks in the band, the answer shows evidence of reading beyond the specification requirements.

(A/B) 16-20 Marks

A well-constructed essay that includes all of the points that could be expected of a good candidate.

The response links several topics to the main theme of the question that form a series of interrelated points which are clearly explained.

The Biology is fundamentally correct A-level content. It contains some detailed points, though there may be some that are less well developed, with appropriate use of terminology.

Perhaps there is one significant error and/or one irrelevant topic that detracts from the overall quality of the answer.

(B/C) 11-15 Marks

Includes a number of key ideas but they are not specifically tailored to the question and there are some errors of detail.

The response mostly deals with suitable topics, but they are not interrelated and links are not made to the theme of the question.

The Biology is usually correct A-level content, though it lacks detail. Generally, it is clearly explained and uses the appropriate terminology.

Some significant errors and/or more than one irrelevant topic.

(D) 6-10 Marks

A very superficial essay that maybe relates to one or two topics related to the title, but not in any real depth.

The response predominantly deals with only one or two topics related to the question.

The Biology presented shows some superficial A-level content that may be poorly explained, lacks sufficient detail or shows a limited use of appropriate terminology.

May contain a number of significant errors and/or irrelevant topics.

(E/U) 1-5 Marks

Nothing more than a list of facts, some of which might be relevant.

The response only indirectly addresses the theme of the question and merely presents a series of biological facts that are usually descriptive in nature or poorly explained and may also be factually incorrect at times.

The content and terminology are generally below A-level.

May contain a large number of errors and/or irrelevant topics.

Without reading these in great depth, we can see that a good essay is not only factually correct, but is also relevant and specific to the title. As well as showing the correct use of terminology, each paragraph relates directly back to the title and adds something to the discussion.

Therefore, a title, such as 'The Importance of Movement', doesn't mean 'tell us everything about movement'. If you did that, it that would get a B/C. However, if you wrote about movement AND WHY IT IS IMPORTANT, it would take that same essay up to an A. The change in grade isn't due to more revision or practice, but just answering the question!

What topics come up?

Now we have seen what the examiners are looking for in your essay, we need to know what essay titles are the most common? In the past 20 years, the overwhelming majority of titles have either a biochemical or ecological stem. This certainly does not mean that a good essay is limited, and it should also incorporate some genetics or physiology, but the starting point is with a molecule or process. I have listed below what topics I might be referring to as a 'stem'.

1. Biochemistry and cells:
   Proteins, carbohydrates, water, lipids, membranes, 'shape', structure and function, immunology and disease and enzymes.
2. Ecology:
   Energy transfer and cycles (including the role of certain elements in living organisms).
3. Other, a bit of catch-all as few titles do not have some element of biochemistry as a stem. There are a few examples, namely: Physiology & organisms – Digestion, negative feedback, diseases, homeostasis. Also Genetics and DNA – Structure, mitosis, meiosis and protein synthesis to genetic manipulation and stem cells.

In the exam, you will be offered two titles. It is important that you choose the one that you think offers the most marks, not the one that looks the most interesting/easy. This will be based on your confidence in the different topics. However, there will almost always be a biochemistry or cells essay amongst them. I have already written about how to approach these in an exam. The first thing you should do is look at them, so you can keep modifying your essay plan as you attempt the other questions.

But how do I learn 40 essays?

You don't. Rather you read them and take note of their style and content, and then use this as a starter to writing your own. If writing an A* essay is a ten-step process, this book gets you to about the seventh step in a short time. However, you can't take this book into an exam, open it and then copy down the essay. Rather, you need to be able to construct your own essay on your own.

Below is an example title:

The importance of *proteins* in living organisms.

Although this looks uninviting and vague, it is fantastic news as there are lots to write about and a good number of 'model paragraphs' that can be fitted together. Any title that starts with 'the importance of' needs half a side of simple AS describing the molecule AND NO MORE. Again, the question here is the importance of something, not an invitation to write down everything you know about it.

The aim of this book is not to be a revision guide on what a protein is, as something such as CGP will be far more appropriate. However, we will look at how to incorporate some of the higher value A2 knowledge into your essay.

A great topic to incorporate is the Electron Transport Chain and Light Dependent Reactions. This is great for marks as it is an A2 topic, so it will be fresh in your memory, has lots of excellent specific vocab and can be put with almost any essay in biochemistry – proteins, enzymes, membranes (and therefore lipids) or carbohydrates (or concentration gradients/diffusion), even water and oxygen. I will put two copies below: the first is for the title 'the importance of proteins', and the second for the title 'the importance of membranes'. In the second, I have highlighted the differences to make sure they answer the specific title. Look to see what the differences are and make the answer relevant, but you should also see how similar they are. Notice how I have added the name of cytochrome oxidase to show my additional reading, even though I might not really know what it is!

The electron transport chain is found on the folded inner membrane of mitochondria. It is composed of a series of electron carrier proteins (also known as cytochromes) and has the role of converting the chemical energy in the reduced electron carriers (NADH and FADH), formed during glycolysis, the link reaction and Kreb's cycle into a proton gradient across the inner membrane between the inter-membrane space and the matrix of the mitochondria. The role of the electron carrier proteins on the inner membrane is to oxidise the NADH/FADH to form NAD + H^+ and a free electron, which is taken up by the cytochrome. The electron then travels along the electron carrier chain losing energy as it does, which is transferred into pumping protons across the membrane from the matrix into the inter-membrane space. When the electron gets to the terminal electron carrier protein (cytochrome oxidase), it binds with oxygen and protons to form water ($4H^+ + O_2 + 4e^- \rightarrow 2H_2O$). This forms a concentration and electro-chemical gradient between the inter-membrane space and the matrix. The protons move through a transmembrane protein, which acts as an enzyme called ATP synthetase. As the protons move through the enzyme it catalyses the reaction ADP + $P_i \rightarrow$ ATP. Without the proteins present in the membrane, the mitochondria would not be able to form ATP and aerobic respiration would not occur.

If I was to rewrite this paragraph for the importance of membranes, I would change it so that it read like this. I have highlighted in bold the changes required to make it specific to the title, but see how much is the same and A* standard.

The electron transport chain is found on the inner membrane of mitochondria. It is composed of a series of electron carrier proteins (also known as cytochromes) and has the role of converting the chemical energy in the reduced electron carriers (NADH and FADH) that are formed during glycolysis, the link reaction and Kreb's cycle into a proton gradient across the inner membrane between the inter-membrane space and the matrix of the mitochondria. The role of the electron carrier proteins on the inner membrane is to oxidise the NADH/FADH to form $NAD + H^+$ and a free electron, which is taken up by the cytochrome. The electron then travels along the electron carrier chain, losing energy as it does, which is transferred into pumping protons across the membrane from the matrix into the inter-membrane space. When the electron gets to the terminal electron carrier protein (cytochrome oxidase) it binds with oxygen and protons to form water ($4H^+ + O_2 + 4e^- \rightarrow 2H_2O$). This forms a concentration and electro-chemical gradient between the inter-membrane space and the matrix **across the membrane**. The protons move through a transmembrane protein that acts as an enzyme called ATP synthetase. As the protons move through the enzyme, it catalyses the reaction ADP $+ P_i \rightarrow$ ATP. Without **the two membranes and the proteins located on them**, the mitochondria would not be able to form ATP and aerobic respiration would not occur. **The folding of the inner membrane increases the surface area, so more electron carrier chains can be present, increasing the amount of ATP that can be formed.**

Again, with a number of small changes, this paragraph can be changed to 'the importance of enzymes' etc. Therefore, rather than learn a series of essays in the hope that one may turn up, it is better to grasp a number of paragraphs and then use them whenever possible to make a number of modifications. As your teacher gives you feedback on each essay, don't do the natural thing of looking at the mark and not reflecting on it. Rather, use previous essays as building blocks to the next. I hope that you can start at a higher level by using the A* essays here and then use them as a basis for other titles. However, if there is any content you are unsure of, DO LOOK IT UP in a revision guide.

This book is a great addition to your preparation, as it will show you the level and construction that you are aiming for. However, you do need to have an idea of what you are writing. As all these essays are real, you will see that there is a variety of styles and emphasis. Rest assured, all are of a top standard, but it reinforces what they have in common. One problem with a book of this type is the order the essays are put in. I have tried my best to put them in some logical order, but as good essays have a range of different aspects there are some topics that might crop up more than once in different areas of the book. This is unavoidable but I am sure you will appreciate why it occurs.

BIOCHEMISTRY AND CELLS

How these AS topics relate to different areas of the specification are summarised below.

Title content	Parts of specification
Proteins	Structure, haemoglobin, enzymes (linking to respiration/electron transport chain), membrane channels – nerve cells, glycoproteins, antibodies, muscles, insulin/glucagon, receptors.
Enzymes	Structure and synthesis, factors affecting them, digestion, metabolic pathways and negative feedback, electron transport chain, photosynthesis, DNA (either within a cell or in genetic engineering, dependent on the question). Other examples, if there's time – nerves and muscles.
Carbohydrates	Structure, respiration and photosynthesis, glycoproteins (antigens), cellulose, starch.
Lipids	Structure, energy, phospholipids, membranes – see below.
Membranes	Structure, transport proteins,

	glycoproteins, electron transport chain, photosynthesis, nerves and muscles. If question allows, internal membranes for the nucleus, R.E.R. and Golgi apparatus.
Shape	Enzymes – with examples from above, antigens, antibodies and DNA/protein synthesis.

You will see there are a number of topics in the chart above that can be fitted into a number of essay titles. We start building our 'perfect paragraph' toolbox by choosing some of these topics and writing a paragraph plan for each. I suggest that if you are reading the e-book you highlight these so that when you have finished, they will all be kept together at the end for revision.

Molecules

The building blocks of Biology are the molecules from which everything is made. This is why you spent half a term looking at their structures at the start of year 12 and their roles in year 13. As they are spread across so many units, they are a great basis for a question and definitely one topic to prepare for. Although the role of carbohydrates or proteins in a question looks dull, it is great for securing marks. The following titles and similar variations have been set over the years and each will be analysed. It is interesting that water and inorganic ions have been added as new topics for 2017. Therefore, these are excellent candidates to be an essay title. Therefore, I have added an essay on each, even though there is no past paper essay to base mine on.

So let us look at our first title. Here, I will go through how this essay was constructed and why. I won't go into this level of detail for all the essays, but it is essential that at this stage you understand the process.

The structure and functions of carbohydrates

The first thing that I would do when planning for this essay is think in terms of topics. You studied the structure of carbohydrates in year 12 and there is quite a bit that could be used here. However, being an AS topic, I would limit this to a side tops. The topics to consider are listed below. These are taken from the mark scheme published by AQA. All topics are listed for all the essay titles. However, as we have seen, you will only get a high mark if you focus on around 4 in detail, focusing in particular on A2, rather than just brush over them all.

Start with AS topics:

Draw the structure of α-glucose.
Table showing the monomers within disaccharides and where found.
Condensation and hydrolysis.
Then, focus on the function of these: soluble, blood and digestion, phloem.
Don't forget plants and bacteria.
Polysaccharides – amylose & amylopectin structure and role. Helix, compact, insoluble – osmosis, branching. Glycogen, liver and muscles.
Cellulose – structure and function, β-glucose, h-bonds, microfibrils. Rigid.
Cell walls in bacteria made of murein.
Immunology – antigens are often glycoproteins (this wasn't in the mark scheme one year, but it's always interesting).

Then, think about A2 topics:

Respiration - Glucose: a source of energy; a substrate in aerobic and anaerobic respiration; biochemistry of aerobic respiration (brief outline).

Photosynthesis - Light-independent reactions: the formation of carbohydrates, carbon dioxide accepted by RBP, reduction of glycerate-3-phosphate to carbohydrate, and regeneration of RBP.

Homeostasis - Importance of the control of blood glucose.

Genetics – actually, this is not only relevant work in AS, but also genetics as A2, due to the amount of time spent on it. Pentoses: Deoxyribose / Ribose in DNA / RNA – phosphodiester bonds provide strength and their roles in transcription and translation.

So how would this essay look? It is easy to look at the topics above and think, great there is loads on AS, so it will be easy. However, remember it is important to make sure there is a good range and to get a good amount of A2 in here (as a rule of thumb, two-thirds). The other danger is that you will start writing and forgetting that the title is specifically the structure and function, rather than the making of, etc. Below is an essay I have put together that would get more than 22 out of 25. The introduction is simply a vague outline of my essay plan and the conclusion will be a summary. In terms of the introductions and conclusions, I tell my pupils to remember this – **tell me what you're going to tell me** (introduction) tell me (the body of the essay) and tell me what you've told me (conclusion):

The structure and functions of carbohydrates

Carbohydrates have a range of roles in living organisms. This range is possible due to the diverse range of structures and, therefore, properties they have. Below I will start by discussing the simple soluble mono- and disaccharides and then talk about the more complex polysaccharides. They are also a component of nucleotides and present as glycoproteins on membranes.

The most common carbohydrate in living organisms is α-glucose. It is formed in the light independent reaction of photosynthesis and used in both aerobic and anaerobic respiration. Its structure is below.

Draw a picture here, if you know it.

α-glucose is a monosaccharide. This is because it is a singular sugar unit that is not bound to another. Monosaccharides are able to join together via condensation reactions. In a condensation reaction, the OH groups on the carbon 1 of one glucose molecule and the carbon 4 of a second react to produce water as a waste product, and then the remaining oxygen joins the two monosaccharides together with an ester bond, which in the case of carbohydrates is also known as a glycosidic bond. If two α-glucose molecules were to join together, as above, the bond would be known as an α-1,4-glycosidic bond and form maltose, which is the sugar found in grains. Monosaccharides can come in a range of structural isomers. In the case of glucose, above, it has the molecular formula $C_6H_{12}O_6$. Other monosaccharides with the same molecular formula, but different structures, are fructose and galactose. These can bind with α-glucose to form the disaccharides sucrose and lactose, respectively. Mono- and disaccharides have similar roles to each other due to their physical properties. They are soluble, so are often used to transport 'energy' around the body, such as glucose in the blood. Glucose formed during photosynthesis is turned into sucrose, which can then dissolve in water and go down the phloem in plants. Lactose is present in breast milk, enabling energy to be passed to the baby from the mother, where it can then be hydrolysed to break the glycosidic bond with the enzymic addition of water. This solubility, however, can also cause osmotic problems, which is why it needs to be converted into an insoluble form when it is to be stored for long periods of time.

There is a range of different polysaccharides that have different functions linked to their structures. There are two isomers of starch, amylose and amylopectin. Amylose is the simpler of the two, consisting of a long chain of α-glucose molecules, joined by α-1,4-glycosidic bonds. This raps into a helical shape due to hydrogen bonds forming between the glucose molecules. This structure helps it to be compact, which is important in its role, yet it is large enough to not pass through the membranes. Also, as it is large, it is insoluble and so is osmotically neutral. Again, this is important in storing a large amount of glucose in tubers and other organs as it stops the cell bursting. Amylopectin has the same basic structure as amylose; however, it also has a number of α-1,6-glycosidic bonds that result in branching. This means there are more exposed glucose molecules on the molecule. Therefore, if respiration needs to happen quickly, more glucose can be hydrolysed from the starch molecule per second. This is a great example of how, in evolution, structure has adapted to function.

Glycogen is present in animal muscle and liver cells and has a similar structure to amylopectin. However, as respiration is required at a faster rate in mammals, it has far more branches so that the glucose can be hydrolysed from the glycogen at an even quicker rate. It is important to control the concentration of glucose in the blood, as not only could it cause osmotic damage to cells, but it can also cause diabetes. If there is too much glucose in the blood, the water potential of blood is reduced to a point where water molecules diffuse out of cells into the blood by osmosis. the, if it is too low, cells are unable to carry out normal activities due to lack of respiration. This is controlled by hormones produced by the islets of Langerhans within the pancreas called insulin and glucagon by negative feedback.

In plants, cellulose is a second polymer of glucose, but this time of the β-structural isomer. At the carbon 1 of the glucose molecule, the OH group is angled upwards rather than down, as in α-glucose. This means that the resultant β-1,4-glucose causes the glucose molecules to alternate their rotation, causing long straight chains to form. The alternating also means that animals are unable to digest the cellulose. Ruminant animals are able to by having symbiotic bacteria in their gut. Being large they are also insoluble, so that they are able to act as a strong cell wall. The OH groups within the chains link with other chains to form microfibrils. Layers of these fibrils are orientated in different directions and interwoven and bedded in a matrix. This ensures that the cell wall is not only is rigid, but also permeable.

Carbohydrates don't only have storage and structural functions. Nucleotides of both DNA and RNA have pentose sugars attached to nucleic acids and phosphate groups. The structural difference is the absence of an oxygen atom on the second carbon in deoxyribose, when compared to ribose. However, they have a similar role in providing strength in the sugar-phosphate backbone, as phosphodiester bonds form between the pentose sugar and the phosphate group of another nucleotide. The resultant polymers, of which the pentose sugars are an essential part, are used in chromosomes (deoxyribose) and RNA (ribose).

Glucose is formed by photosynthesis, and the energy of a photon of light is converted into the chemical energy within a covalent bond. In the light independent stage of this reaction, which occurs in the stroma, Ribulose-*bis*-phosphate is used as the substrate in the Calvin Cycle. This is a 5 carbon sugar and the addition of a sixth carbon derived from carbon dioxide by the enzyme RuBISCO forms two molecules of glycerate-3-phosphate. These, in turn, are reduced to form triose phosphate, which are both 3 carbon molecules. The function of triose phosphate is it can be used as the building blocks for further organic molecules, such as glucose and amino acids. However, some of it is recycled to form more ribulose-*bis*-phosphate which can then re-join the Calvin Cycle.

In the essay above, I have linked the structure of carbohydrates to their function. It is the bonding within carbohydrates that either gives them their structural stability in the case of cellulose and deoxyribose, or ability to store and transfer energy in the case of respiration and photosynthesis. As such, carbohydrates have been essential from the very beginning for the evolution of life.

The importance of shapes fitting together in cells and organisms

1) Carbohydrates – storage / structural / glycoprotein etc.
2) Proteins – levels of structure / enzymes – specificity / properties
3) Lipids – phospholipids
4) Interaction with receptors
5) Drugs
6) Antibodies (antibody – antigen complex)
7) Hormones – seconds messenger / direct action
8) Neurotransmitters – synapses

The 3D shape of molecules is essential, not only for the functions of proteins, but also the storage and roles of carbohydrates. Various molecules have to be complementary to each other; for example, a receptor site or an enzyme. In this essay, I will discuss examples and stress how the shape is important for their role.

The predominant importance of shapes fitting together in a complementary fashion is the formation of enzyme-substrate complexes. The initial hypothesis of how enzymes were stimulated by substrates was the lock and key hypothesis, that only one specific molecule could bind to an enzyme. However, the more recently accepted hypothesis is that of the induced fit hypothesis. This is because it was found that similar molecules could still be complementary and bind to the active site region of an enzyme, thereby forming an enzyme-substrate complex.

As this complex is made, it allows a conformational change, which means that the reaction can occur by reducing the activation energy. The reason that enzymes can be so adaptable and specific in their shape is due to the variation that can be produced in their structure. The tertiary and quaternary structures can be rigid due to disulphide bonds between cysteines and other intermolecular bonds, such as hydrogen bonds and van der Walls forces. However, they can also be flexible, as in the case of keratin. The shapes that can form in these active sites allow reactions to occur that otherwise would not.

These active sites can also act as targets for drugs and inhibitors. Drugs will often work as competitive or non-competitive inhibitors to enzymes of bacteria. As a result, their shape is either similar to the substrate and can, therefore, occupy the active site or – as in the case of a non-competitive inhibitor – bind to an allosteric site and, therefore, change the shape of the active site, stopping the reaction occurring. This is important because they allow bodies to regulate the enzymes action as in negative feedback and nerves or for treatment as in the case of antibiotics working on the enzymes that make the murein walls of bacteria.

The specific shapes of enzymes in plants are essential for photosynthesis to occur. For example, the enzyme rubisco has a specific shape in the light independent stages of photosynthesis that allows it to fixate carbon dioxide with ribulose bisphosphate to form two molecules of glycerate-

3-phosphate. The enzyme is acting as a biological catalyst, as it is allowing an otherwise kinetically stable reaction to take place at relatively low temperatures. This is because of the specificity of the active site, which is complementary to the RuBP and CO_2 substrates, thereby allowing it to form an enzyme substrate complex.

The shape of polysaccharides also has an interesting factor in the ability of organisms to digest them. β-glucose, as found in cellulose, has an alternating shape. The OH groups on either side are on opposite directions and therefore the 1,4-glycosidic bond that forms cause the glucose molecules to be opposite each other. This makes it indigestible to mammals, as they don't have enzymes that are complementary to this shape. However, bacteria do and this is why they can live in a symbiotic relationship with ruminants.

Adrenaline is a hormone that is produced by the adrenal glands. Its shape is specific and complementary to that of the G-protein receptor found on muscle tissue. Once bound, it causes the $G\alpha$'s subunit to be released that, when GTP binds, activates the adenylyl cyclase enzyme. This causes the conversion of ATP into cAMP. The cAMP has a specific shape complementary to the inhibitor region complexes bound to protein kinase A. As the cAMP binds to the inhibitor region, it releases and activates the protein kinase A that then, in a cascade reaction, activates various other enzymes involved in glycogenolysis and gluconeogenesis. The complementary nature of these shapes allows the formation of secondary pathways that allow the control of molecular signalling. Drugs with a similar shape to the neurotransmitters can completely block these binding sites and this is how they have their effect.

The specificity of shapes is also important in protecting the human body against the invasion of pathogens in the secondary immune response. This is because T-lymphocytes can recognise pathogens as being foreign due to the surface antigens. The T-lymphocytes that have specific shapes to the antigen on the pathogen will sensitise via the release of interleukins to the specific B-cells. The sensitised B-cells then divide into B-memory cells and B-plasma cells. These B-plasma cells release antibodies that have specific complementary shapes to the antigens on the pathogen, and can thus form antigen-antibody complexes. As the antibodies have 2 antigen binding sites on their quaternary structure, it allows the agglutination of pathogens, which increases the efficiency of phagocytosis.

Shape is also an essential part of the structure and function of the DNA molecule. For example, the winding shape of the double helix helps to protect the nitrogenous bases from biochemical attack. Furthermore, the specific shapes of the bases allow it to form specific complementary base pairs, where adenine forms 2 hydrogen bonds with thymine and guanine forms 3 hydrogen bonds with cytosine. This specific base pairing is an essential part of semi-conservative DNA replication. In this, only complementary bases can join via hydrogen bonding and, therefore, ensure the accuracy of either replication or transcription and translation in protein synthesis.

Specific shapes must also fit together to allow the propagation of a nervous impulse across a synapse. It is important that the neurotransmitter released from the pre-synaptic terminal only binds to specific receptor sites on the post-synaptic terminal, thereby only causing depolarisation of the post-synaptic membrane. This ensures uni-directionality of the nervous impulse. Furthermore, the shape of the neurotransmitter and the enzyme that breaks it down must also be specific. For example, at a cholinergic synapse, the acetylcholineesterase must have a specific complementary shape to the acetylcholine neurotransmitter, so that it can form an enzyme substrate complex and thus break it down in a hydrolysis reaction. This ensures electrical impulses aren't fired in the absence of a stimulus.

In conclusion, the importance of shapes fitting together is essential for all life, particularly on a molecular level as it allows for specificity and communication. Without the shapes of these molecules, reactions and interactions wouldn't occur between organisms and their environment and would, therefore, life would not be able to exist.

There has also been a previous title that was very similar – 'The importance of molecular shape.' As this is essentially the same title, you could submit the same essay. Another similar title is *below. The essay that follows got a low A*. Notice that he has not included everything, but more than enough in considerable depth.*

<u>Polymers have different structures. They also have different functions. Describe how the structures of different polymers are related to their functions.</u>

1) Biological molecules, carbohydrates and proteins
2) The release of energy from carbohydrate
3) The control of blood glucose
4) Enzymes
5) DNA as genetic material, structure of nucleic acids
6) Principles of immunology
7) The transport of respiratory gases
8) Cell ultrastructure, cell walls
9) Biological molecules, carbohydrates and proteins

Polymers are long chain molecules made up of individual monomers that have been joined together in some type of reaction. Not only are polymers an important part of the structure and ultrastructure of cells, but they play an important role in genetics, in the form of DNA and RNA.

The individual units, or monomers, usually undergo a condensation reaction in order to form a (covalent) bond. In this type of polymerisation reaction, a small, simple molecule is lost from the monomers, and in biological polymers, the molecule that is lost is usually water. Conversely, the bond between monomers is broken by a hydrolysis reaction, in which water is added across the bond.

DNA and RNA are both good examples of polymers. Each monomer is made up of a nitrogenous base, a sugar (either ribose or deoxyribose) and a phosphate group. In DNA, the nitrogenous bases are adenine, thymine, cytosine and guanine, and in RNA the thymine is swapped for uracil. DNA exists naturally as a double helix, and the phosphate group of one nucleotide forms a bond with the sugar of an adjacent nucleotide to form a phosphodiester bond. These bonds mean that the double helix has a deoxyribose-phosphate backbone. This is advantageous because it means that there is a lower probability of the DNA being corrupted since it is negatively charged (due to the phosphate group) and is hydrophilic. Furthermore, the fact that it exists as a double helix with two strands (the sense and antisense strands) allows for semi-conservative replication. This means that the helix separates (using DNA helicase) and each strand acts as a template, to which free floating DNA nucleotides can bind and form a new strand of DNA. Semi-conservative replication is advantageous since it significantly lowers the risk of a mutation, which could alter the structure and, therefore, the function that the gene codes for. It is important to maintain the integrity of DNA and that it replicates accurately because mutations which alter the sequence of bases can lead to the production of non-functional proteins, and these proteins may have some survival value to the organism.

RNA is different to DNA in that it is single stranded and

uses uracil, instead of thymine. The reason for using thymine, rather than uracil in DNA, is that cytosine can spontaneously react to form uracil and this mistake would be more difficult to correct in DNA, whereas RNA has a relatively short lifespan compared to DNA, so the change would not have as much impact. Messenger RNA (mRNA) is single stranded and is significantly shorter than DNA because it has undergone a process called splicing. In this, non-coding sections of pre-mRNA (i.e. introns) are removed. This is a fundamental difference between the structure of DNA and mRNA because the ribosomes cannot translate the mRNA if there are introns present.

Glucose is an extremely important molecule in living organisms and it can be used in several different polymerisation reactions to form different polymers, which have very different structures and functions. In plants, an example of this is starch, which is comprised of amylose and amylopectin. Amylose is a straight chain molecule and the alpha (D) glucose molecules are bonded together by α-1,4-glycosidic bonds. On the other hand, amylopectin is much more branched than amylose, as it contains both 1,4 and 1,6 glycosidic bonds. Whilst both amylose and amylopectin are found in starch, it is noteworthy that amylose is more efficiently stored, since its straight chain can be easily coiled and amylopectin provides a more immediate source of energy because it is more easily hydrolysed by enzymes. A further example of a glucose-based polymer in plants is cellulose, which provides structural support to plant cells, as a part of the cell wall. The monomer for this polymer is beta glucose, and this means that the chains of cellulose have an alternating structure, with each glucose molecule rotated by 180 degrees, compared to the adjacent molecules. The chains of cellulose form hydrogen bonds and, although these are weak, there are many of them.

Glucose can also form polymers in animals. In fact, animals rely on the ability to form polymers from glucose, as a physiological mechanism to enable homeostatic control of their blood glucose concentration. When the blood glucose concentration is too high, the beta cells of the pancreas secrete an increased concentration of insulin into the blood. These bind to specific receptors on the cell surface membrane of cells. As a result, it stimulates adenylate cyclase to convert ATP into cyclic AMP, which activates specific enzymes to polymerise glucose molecules and store them as glycogen, an insoluble polymer. As a result, the blood glucose concentration falls and the amount of insulin secreted by the pancreas also falls due to a negative feedback loop. Like amylopectin, glycogen is a branched polysaccharide and so when glucose is required – for example, for respiration – glucose can easily be removed from the branches by enzymes.

Perhaps the most important polymers in any biological organism are proteins. The monomer of a protein (or polypeptide) is an amino acid. The carboxyl group of one amino acid can form an amide (i.e. a peptide) bond with the amine group of another amino acid and during this condensation reaction, a molecule of water is removed. As lots of amino acids join and form peptide bonds, a polypeptide is formed. Each polypeptide has a very specific primary structure (i.e. sequence of amino acids.) The amino acids in the polypeptide interact with one another by forming hydrogen, ionic and disulphide bonds. Consequently, the polypeptide will fold into a very specific 3D shape and its shape will be essential for its function. An example would be enzymes. Due to a specific 3D shape, the active site of an enzyme is very specific and will be complementary to a single substrate. For example, the enzyme acetylcholinesterase is responsible for the breakdown of the neurotransmitter acetylcholine into choline and acetic (ethanoic) acid. Acetylcholinesterase cannot and will not catalyse the breakdown of any other compounds because it cannot form an enzyme-substrate complex with other molecules, due to the specificity of the active site.

In conclusion, polymers play a vital role in many aspects of biology, including significant roles in genetics, in the form of DNA and RNA, as well as providing structural support for cells and storage. Many of the polymers are made up of different monomers, and as such the structures and functions of each of them vary greatly, but they all have different features which make them suited to their functions.

Another related title, which leads on to another topic, is anything to do with bonding. Below is an essay on hydrogen bonding that got an A*. However, I have modified it to add some new additional content on water for the new specification.

<u>The importance of hydrogen bonds in living organisms</u>

1) The passage of water through a plant and cohesion tension
2) The structure of proteins, starch and cellulose
3) Enzymes
4) DNA as genetic material, structure of nucleic acids
5) Gene technology

Hydrogen bonds are important throughout living organisms, existing between many different types of molecule, from those between nitrogenous bases in DNA to those within the secondary structure of proteins, as well as between water molecules. In this essay, I will review not only where they are found, but also how they are essential for the function of living organisms.

Hydrogen bonds are weak and formed between hydrogen atoms and other atoms, normally oxygen, which are nevertheless cumulatively strong. For example, they form between water molecules in the process of cohesion tension, which occurs in plants during transpiration, the process of passage of water up the xylem. Therefore, as the water molecules are bonded together when water leaves through the top of the plant – both by being used in the photolysis of water in photosynthesis and by diffusing out through the stomata in transpiration, which are left open for gas exchange –

water is pulled up the plant to replace it. In addition, some hydrogen bonds are formed between the water and the xylem wall, aiding transfer up, which is called adhesion. These are useful in that they allow more water, necessary for photosynthesis, to reach the leaves where photosynthesis occurs. Sometimes this mass transport can move over tens of metres and therefore without it, plants would not be able to photosynthesise and survive.

The strength of hydrogen bonds is also important in their roles within the structure of different polymers. In cellulose, for example, the structural component of plants' cell walls, long straight chains of beta-glucose are held together by a very large number of hydrogen bonds, making very strong fibres. Similarly, hydrogen bonds exist between sections of starch, a different plant carbohydrate made of alpha-glucose formed into straight amylose and branched amylopectin molecules, making it a structurally strong store of food. Also, these molecules do not cause osmotic problems as they are large and insoluble. Proteins, as well as carbohydrates, have hydrogen bonding within them too. This helps to make up their fixed structures that are important to their function. Hydrogen bonds occur both in the secondary structure, causing localised features of alpha-helixes and beta-pleated sheets, and in the tertiary structure, forming the overall shape of the protein by connecting more distant sections.

This is particularly important in enzymes, where shape is essential, as each enzyme in the active site has a very specific shape that is complementary to its substrate. Earlier described as lock and key, but now accepted as a more induced fit model, this specificity is due to the structure, which ensures that metabolic pathways are maintained. As enzymes control all metabolic reactions within the body, such as essential coenzymes in respiration or rubisco, which fixes carbon to RuBP in the light-independent reaction of photosynthesis, it is very important that these shapes remain intact. Otherwise, if the hydrogen bonds are broken and the enzyme denatures, these reactions cannot occur properly. Denaturation can be caused by changes in pH, with acids (containing H+ ions) or alkalis (containing OH- ions) binding to either part of the hydrogen bond respectively, and so preventing the bonds themselves from forming, as well as by temperature. Many organisms, therefore, resist these changes to avoid the breaking of hydrogen bonds, such as through homeostatic control of temperature at a fixed level in endotherms, which shows how important the bonds are.

Hydrogen bonds can also be found in genetics, as this is how nitrogenous bases bond together – cytosine with guanine, and adenine with thymine in DNA or uracil in RNA. DNA has a two-strand structure, with two sugar phosphate backbones attached to bases and bonds between each strand. The fact that these bases bind together is crucial in genetics – for example, this is required in transcription, as mRNA is formed when RNA polymerase attaches RNA nucleotides together, after they have bound to complementary base pairs on the DNA.

Similarly, DNA replication occurs in the cell cycle after the two strands have been split and new complementary strands are formed by complementary base pairing. This is also relevant in gene technology, such as in the polymerase chain reaction, which is essentially an artificial version of DNA replication, but of one specific gene. After a high temperature has been used to split the hydrogen bonds, primers attach to either side of the gene, and DNA polymerase attaches to this and moves along the enclosed section of DNA, lining up and connecting complementary DNA nucleotides, which form hydrogen bonds with the existing strand. This "in vitro gene cloning" is very useful in providing lots of copies of a gene, which may be required, for example, in DNA fingerprinting, and relies on hydrogen bonds in order to occur correctly.

Therefore, without hydrogen bonding it is unlikely that life would exist and definitely not as we know it. From the intramolecular level within the active sites of enzymes to the mass transport through plants, it is key for the continuation of life on this planet.

Water is a new topic that has entered the specification. Therefore, it would not be surprising to see an essay based around it, as it opens up so many parts of the specification. I have written an essay which I think would score highly. Like all good essays it has the stem of water running through it, so that it answers the question, but also finds opportunities to show a range and content from parts of the specification, but mainly A2. It will come as no surprise that our favourite topics of respiration and photosynthesis make an appearance!

The importance of water in organisms

Life on Earth began in the oceans. The chemical and physical properties of water, which I will explore below, will show how it was able to help support life. Today, even land living organisms like ourselves are predominantly made of water. Within the cell, it takes part directly in many reactions as either a substrate or product. It is also used more generally within homeostasis, sweating, and both as a main constituent in blood plasma and sap in mass transport.

Water is a major constituent of cells. It has several properties that are important in biology. In particular, water is a metabolite in many chemical reactions. At the most basic level, it is a product in condensation reactions. These anabolic reactions are involved in the building up of polymers. Three examples are the formation of glycosidic bonds in carbohydrates, such as maltose from two α-glucose molecules, peptide bonds from two amino acids and ester bonds via the addition of fatty acids to glycerol. When these bonds are broken by hydrolysis, water is released as a waste product.

At a cellular level, water causes phospholipids to form the bilayer found in membranes. Water is a dipolar molecule. The hydrophilic heads of the phospholipids are polar so they can come into contact with the water, whereas the hydrophobic fatty acids are repelled. As a result, the hydrophobic fatty acids 'hide' inside the bilayer, with the phosphate heads being external. This is important because every life form, from the earliest point of evolution, needs to have its own internal environment. With membranes cells and organelles can undertake processes such as chemiosmosis as a proton gradient can form.

This polar nature also allows intermolecular bonds called hydrogen bonds to form between water molecules. These bonds give water molecules a higher specific heat capacity than they would otherwise have and can act as a temperature buffer making aquatic ecosystems, in particular, more stable as there are no sudden changes in temperature that there might otherwise be. This hydrogen bonding means that the energy used to break them is significant for evaporation of sweat to occur as it removes energy from the surface of the skin, causing it to cool. This is called the 'latent heat of vaporisation' and again shows why water is essential to organisms, particularly mammals. The hydrogen bonds also allow water to be moved via transpiration in plants, but I will refer to that more when I discuss mass transport later.

Look at the paragraph below. It looks familiar, doesn't it? All I have done is added an extra sentence and suddenly it is relevant.

Water is also vital within the reactions of respiration. The electron transport chain is found on the folded inner membrane of mitochondria. It is composed of a series of electron carrier proteins (also known as cytochromes) and has the role of converting chemical energy in the reduced electron carriers (NADH and FADH) that is formed during glycolysis, the link reaction and Kreb's cycle into a proton gradient across the inner membrane, between the inter-membrane space and the matrix of the mitochondria. The role of the electron carrier proteins on the inner membrane is to oxidise the NADH/FADH to form $NAD + H^+$ and a free electron, which is taken up by the cytochrome. The electron then travels along the electron carrier chain, losing energy as it does, which is transferred into pumping protons across the membrane from the matrix into the inter-membrane space. When the electron gets to the terminal electron carrier protein (cytochrome oxidase) it binds with oxygen and protons to form water ($4H^+ + O_2 + 4e^- \rightarrow 2H_2O$). Without the water that is formed, the electrons would not be able to leave the electron transport chain so the process would stop. This forms a concentration and electro-chemical gradient between the inter-membrane space and the matrix. The protons move through a transmembrane protein, which acts as an enzyme called ATP synthetase. As the protons move through the enzyme it catalyses the reaction $ADP + P_i \rightarrow ATP$.

In a similar way, the photolysis of water at photosystem II (680nm) on the thylakoid membranes ensures that a steady stream of electrons enter the Z-scheme, so NADPH and ATP can be formed. Photons of light are absorbed by the complex, causing the excitation of an electron meaning. If this electron was not replaced the light dependent reactions could not continue and so photosynthesis would grind to a halt. Due to the energy in the light (photo) the bonds within water are broken (lysis) to release electrons:

$$H_2O \rightarrow {}^1/_2O_2 + 2H^+ + 2e^-$$

Without water acting as a substrate in this way, photosynthesis would stop showing how it is vital for all life on Earth.

As well as being directly involved in reactions it is the most common solvent in the world, both externally in rivers and pools and internally in cytoplasms. In fact, around 60% of the human body is water. Due to its polarity, many molecules important for life dissolve in it. It is the major component of the cytoplasm within cells and with the enzymes and substrates dissolved in it, they can diffuse around the cell and come into contact with each other. It also facilitates molecular movement around an organism in mass transport, such as minerals from the roots through the xylem by transpiration or dissolved in the blood plasma. Examples of things that might be dissolved are soluble products of digestion, such as glucose or amino acids, as well as ions such as Na^+. In both cases, if water was not involved in mass flow, leaves could not get nitrates from the soil to form proteins and sucrose would not go down the phloem to the roots. In animals, the blood plasma transports the products of digestion to where it is needed in cells, and CO_2 dissolves in it and is returned to the lungs.

As can be seen in the essay above, water is fundamental in almost all aspects of life. Without it, life would never have begun and it one of the first molecules that scientists try to detect on planets and moons to see if there is maybe evidence of life.

Another molecule that is easy to overlook, but can turn up, is ATP. This essay was asked a few years ago.

The different ways in which organisms use ATP

1) The nature of ATP and its importance as energy currency in cells.
2) Production of ATP in cytoplasm and mitochondria; aerobic respiration.
3) Anaerobic respiration; role of chloroplasts in ATP production (photophosphorylation).
4) Uses – active transport; maintaining resting potential; reabsorption in nephron; absorption ion the gut; Calvin cycle; muscle contraction; biosynthesis (e.g. protein synthesis) contractile vacuoles.
5) ATP is involved in a large number of anabolic (building up) and physiological processes.

ATP stands for adenosine triphosphate and is the primary source of metabolic energy in cells. It is a good energy source because of the instability of the tertiary phosphodiester bond, which allows it to break down easily in a single step reaction. This enables it to rapidly phosphorylate other molecules with relative ease. It is small and soluble, which means it can be transported around the cell and does not pass out of the cell. It is always available as an immediate source of energy releasing energy in small manageable amounts and can be hydrolysed in a single step reaction by the enzyme ATPase.

Net two ATP molecules are formed during glycolysis in the cytoplasm. Further ATP is formed in mitochondria during aerobic respiration, which occurs during the link reaction and a single molecule directly in the Krebs cycle. Most, however, are formed in the electron transport chain. Here, reducing agents, such as NADH and FADH, formed in the Kreb's cycle, donate electrons to the cytochromes that span the inner membrane and form a proton gradient between the matrix and inter-membrane space. The hydrogen ions diffuse along this gradient through ATP synthetase and ATP is formed from ADP and P_i.

ATP is used in primary active transport to transport molecules from one side of a membrane to another against their concentration gradient. For example, the Na+/K+ pump transports Na+ and K+ ions against their concentration gradient through a carrier protein. The ATP is hydrolysed, thus phosphorylating the carrier protein. This phosphorylation and binding of the Na+ and K+ ions induces a conformational shape change, which transports in the ions against their relative concentration gradients. The bound phosphate group is hydrolysed, thus restoring the carrier protein to its original shape.

All living organisms also use ATP in cell division. The mitosis of a cell, which is useful in both the growth and repair of an organism, uses ATP in anaphase to cause contraction of the spindle fibres. This spindle fibre contraction causes the 2 sister chromatids, attached to one another by the centromere, to separate and be pulled to opposite poles of the cell. After telophase cytokinesis takes place, thus ensuring the 2 daughter cells have identical DNA to the parent cell.

ATP is also quintessential to the secondary messenger model, which is involved in the communication of information within cells. For example, when the adrenaline is bound to the G-protein it causes the $G\alpha$ subunit to be released, which when GTP bound binds and activates the adenylyl cyclase enzyme. This causes the conversion of ATP into cyclic AMP (or cAMP). The cAMP has a specific shape to the inhibitor region complexes bound to protein kinase A. As the cAMP binds to the inhibitor region, it releases and activates the protein kinase A, which then go on in a cascade reaction to activate various other enzymes involved in glycogenolysis and gluconeogenesis.

The contraction of muscle fibres involves the contraction of many sarcomeres made up of myosin and actin. When Ca^{2+} ions are released from the sarcoplasmic reticulum by the arrival of an action potential, it binds to troponin. This causes a conformational change in tropomyosin, causing the exposure of the myosin binding site on the actin. Myosin heads then bind to the actin. In the presence and subsequent hydrolysis of ATP, the bound myosin head undergoes a conformational shape change, causing the power stroke so that the actin filaments are pulled together followed by the release of the ADP. ATP is then attached to the myosin head, which when hydrolysed to

ADP by ATPase provides energy in the recovery stroke of returning the myosin head to the original position, thereby allowing the process to be repeated.

In the light dependent phase of photosynthesis plants generate ATP from the excited electrons formed in photosystem I passing down the electron transport chain in a similar way to that described in mitochondria. This ATP is subsequently used in the light independent stages of photosynthesis for the production of glucose. RuBP a 5-carbon compound is fixated with carbon dioxide by the enzyme rubisco to create 2 molecules of glycerate-3-phosphate. ATP is used along with NADPH to phosphorylate and reduce the 2 molecules of glycerate-3-phosphate into 2 molecules of triose phosphate. The triose phosphates, one every 6 cycles, are used to create a molecule of glucose. The rest of the TP a 3 carbon compound is assimilated together to make RuBP, using ATP as the source of metabolic energy for the bond-making process.

All organisms use ATP in respiration to create more ATP. ATP is used to phosphorylate the glucose into glucose-6-phosphate in glycolysis. The enzyme phosphoglucose isomerase converts the glucose-6-phosphate into fructose-6-phosphate. ATP is then used to phosphorylate fructose-6-phosphate into fructose-1,6-bisphosphate. This breaks down into 2 molecules of triose phosphates, which are then oxidised by the coenzyme NAD and undergo substrate level phosphorylation to create 2 molecules of pyruvate. The pyruvate then goes through the link reaction and subsequently the Krebs cycle, thus reducing NAD and FAD coenzymes. The reduced coenzymes are used in oxidative phosphorylation to produce ATP via chemiosmosis and the help of the ATP synthase, which combines ADP and inorganic phosphate into ATP.

Therefore, we can clearly see that ATP's chemical nature and reactions make it not only a useful immediate energy source, but also absolutely essential for life. It is so essential, in fact, that it is even needed for its own continual formation in glycolysis.

The title above would also lead onto this past paper title:

<u>Inorganic ions include those of sodium, phosphorus and hydrogen. Describe how these and other inorganic ions are used in living organisms.</u>

1) Nitrogen cycles
2) Action potentials and nerve impulses
3) Receptors convert stimuli into electrical impulses
4) Respiration produces ATP which is the immediate form of energy for many cell activities
5) Photosynthesis uses energy from sunlight to synthesise organic molecules from inorganic sources
6) DNA as genetic material
7) Fertilisers and plant growth
8) Hydrogen ions affect pH
9) Factors which affect enzyme action
10) The control of blood pH
11) Digestion in the stomach and small intestine
12) The role of H^+ in respiration & photosynthesis

Inorganic ions are very important in living organisms, and a constant supply of them must be maintained to continue normal function. As well as being directly involved in physiological processes, such as sodium and potassium in action potentials, they are incorporated into important molecules, like phosphorus in ATP, the biological currency of energy.

In terms of their direct use in physiological processes, the ions of sodium and potassium are involved in nerve impulses, with their movement through the neurone membrane creating an action potential. Initially, at resting potential, sodium and potassium are actively exchanged, with potassium entering the neurone and sodium leaving it. As potassium can diffuse back out along its concentration gradient through potassium channels, whereas sodium channels are closed, the outside of the neurone is more positive than the inside, creating a negative potential difference. A stimulus opens sodium channels, causing depolarisation, with sodium re-entering the neurone, until a certain point is reached. The sodium channels then close and potassium channels open, causing repolarisation and eventually hyperpolarisation below the original resting potential, as the potassium channels are slow to close before this section of the neurone returns to resting potential. As some sodium ions diffuse sideways, a wave of depolarisation occurs along the neurone, transmitting an electrical signal, and these two inorganic ions are necessary for this. At the synapses, a third ion is also involved – calcium – which is taken in by the pre-synaptic knob when a stimulus arrives and combines with the vesicles there, causing them to release neurotransmitters into the synaptic cleft. These then diffuse across the synapse and attach to receptors, causing them to take in sodium or chlorine ions and so stimulate or prevent an action potential, respectively.

Calcium is also used as a messenger in muscle cells. When an action potential reaches a muscle cell it causes the release of calcium from the sarcoplasmic reticulum.

These can bind to troponin and cause a change in tropomyocin. This exposes the myosin binding sites in the actin, allowing the contraction of the muscle by the sliding filament model.

Many molecules that are important in biology incorporate inorganic ions too. Phosphorus, for example, can be found in DNA, in the sugar-phosphate backbone. Being the genetic material, DNA is required in all cells to act as the template from which mRNA is transcribed and then used in translation to make a protein the requirement for phosphorus is constant. Add to this semi-conservative replication before mitosis, you can see how there is a high demand for this ion. The structural integrity of DNA and RNA are important and most of this comes from the strong covalent sugar-phosphate bonds that hold the nucleotides together.

Three phosphate groups are found in ATP, which provides the immediate source of energy for all reactions in the body. In fact, it is the removal of the third phosphate group in this molecule that makes ADP and releases this energy in a usefully quick, one-step reaction. ATP is produced by respiration from glucose, with both substrate-level and oxidative phosphorylation making it from ADP and an inorganic phosphate molecule, and it can then be broken down to release energy.

Both respiration and photosynthesis, however, use another inorganic ion – hydrogen. In the light-dependent stage of photosynthesis, the photolysis of water splits up water into oxygen, electrons and hydrogen ions, and the second of these travel along the electron transport chain, providing energy to actively transport hydrogen ions across the thylakoid membrane into the inside of the thylakoid. This creates an electrochemical gradient that the hydrogen ions diffuse along through ATP synthase, creating ATP, which is then used in the light-independent stage of photosynthesis, ultimately to make organic compounds. Similarly, in respiration, the process of oxidative phosphorylation requires that hydrogen ions, which are formed by the oxidation of reduced NAD and FAD, be actively transported across the mitochondrial membrane, before diffusing back through ATP synthase to make ATP.

Hydrogen ions on their own can have a detrimental effect on proteins. Two clear examples of this are involved in the denaturation of their structure. In enzymes, the hydrogen ions interfere with the hydrogen bonding within the secondary and tertiary structures. This disrupts the shape of the active site, so it is no longer complementary to its substrate, slowing down or stopping the reaction from occurring. This can also affect haemoglobin. Haem groups contain iron, which is able to form ligands with oxygen molecules in myoglobin and haemoglobin. In acidic environments, such as in respiring muscles, the affinity for oxygen decreases making it dissociate. This is known as the Bohr effect and, therefore, enables oxygen to be released.

Nitrogen is another inorganic ion used in important molecules, particularly proteins. As in all amino acids, the monomers they are made from, contain nitrogen. This is why growing plants requires a source of nitrogen, unlike animals – that absorb amino acids to make necessary proteins, such as enzymes, by consuming and digesting proteins in other organic matter – they must make their own by absorbing nitrogen in the form of nitrates from the ground. This normally occurs through the nitrogen cycle, the movement of nitrogen through ecosystems. For example, nitrogen fixing bacteria turn atmospheric nitrogen gas into ammonia, which can be used by plants, and nitrates in dead plants and animals are turned into ammonia in ammonification and then nitrites in nitrification. However, nitrogen can also be added artificially to soils, through fertilisers that improve growth, and to increase yield.

As can be seen above, inorganic ions are vital for the functioning of organisms but can easily be overlooked. They are found structurally in molecules, such as DNA, but are also substrates within reactions. Their unique chemical properties are essential for life.

MEMBRANES AND TRANSPORT

When we move out from particular molecules, the next logical topic is organelles. Membranes are a great example of where exam candidates will answer the question they want to be asked, rather than the one that has actually been set. There have been three specific membrane titles so far, but it would be easy to think they were all the same. However, look at their titles closely and see how they vary.

1. The structure and importance of the plasma membranes that are found within and around cells.
2. Describe the structure and function of membranes in organisms.
3. The part played by the movement of substances across cell membranes in the functioning of different organs and organ systems.

The thing to note here, and the common mistake that candidates make, is they see the word membranes and then spend a side talking about mitochondria. This would have been great for the first two titles, but it is not relevant for the last title at all, which specifically talks of 'cell membranes'. This also exposes another flaw that many candidates make, which is to forget the existence of plants.

The mark schemes for the first two titles are very similar:

AS - fluid mosaic model and a diagram of the different types of proteins.

Membranes within cells:
A2 – mitochondria, chloroplasts and also the endoplasmic reticulum in protein synthesis.

Membranes around cells (specifically and correctly referring to (facilitated) diffusion, osmosis and active transport):
AS – absorption through the gut & gas exchange.
A2 – receptors (eye/touch) impulses and synapses and hormone action.

For the second title, it is also possible to discuss prokaryotes.

You can see from these essay plans how I am already thinking in terms of AS and A2. This is because it will give me the spread of topic that I need from the specification to get a top grade. This is how I would suggest you construct your plans, dividing them by units and then key words that will act as a list to help you write the paragraphs you already have in your head.

The third title is far more specific and the examiners reported that many of the candidates completed it poorly. This doesn't make it a bad title, just poorly answered, as the candidates just wrote down all that they knew about membranes without properly reading the question. This is from a 'legacy' paper, therefore the specification was different and the mark scheme contains elements that are no longer in the A-level. I have edited it to make it more relevant, but it is a great example of how to take an essay and make sure that everything is relevant to the specific title. It does not show any knowledge that I would not expect a B grade candidate to have, but it is the way it was written that got it a top mark.

The part played by the movement of substances across cell membranes in the functioning of different organs and organ systems.

Suggested topics.
1) Plasma membranes and movement across
2) Gaseous exchange system/lungs
3) Digestive system/small intestine
4) Blood vascular system
5) Transpiration/root/stem
6) Mass flow/leaf/stem
7) Nervous system/eye
8) Excretory system/kidney
9) Muscle systems
10) Liver, blood glucose
11) Root mineral ions

*In a good essay, the emphasis should be **on movement across membranes** involving organ function. You will notice the essay below does not include many of the above, as only 4 were needed to access full marks.*

The movement of substances across cell membranes is very important in ensuring that life continues, for it allows exchange with the environment outside the cell, whether this be the internal environment of the body or the outside world itself, and this is necessary to keep life going. The existence of a plasma membrane also gives control over what can enter and exit a cell, which is necessary for them to carry out their functions correctly.

The structure of the plasma membrane allows this controlled transfer. It consists of a phospholipid bilayer, with the hydrophilic phosphate heads facing out and the hydrophobic tails facing in, to produce a barrier to large and water-soluble substances, such as sodium ions. Proteins, such as protein channels and carrier proteins, can be found embedded in this bilayer. This is where the term "fluid mosaic" model comes from, with the phospholipids able to move around freely, so that the mosaic pattern of the proteins keeps changing. These proteins allow the transfer of substances into or out of the cell that could otherwise not traverse the barrier – the fact that these must pass through proteins gives control over what enters the cell. Carrier proteins allow large molecules to diffuse across the membrane. Molecules attach to the proteins, causing them to change shape, releasing the molecules on the other side of the membrane. Protein channels allow charged particles to diffuse straight through them, with different ones allowing different particles. This means that different membranes can be selectively permeable via the make-up of the specific protein channels.

One important movement across cell membranes is the absorption of the products of digestion within the small intestine. After large molecules are broken down into their component soluble monomers by enzymes, such as pepsin breaking down proteins into amino acids in the stomach, these smaller products of digestion can be absorbed, so that the body can use them, generally building them back into more complex molecules. One particularly important substance to be absorbed is glucose, which is the primary energy source for the body through aerobic respiration. This initially diffuses across the epithelium into the blood, through plasma membranes, when the concentration is higher in the lumen of the small intestine than in the blood. However, after enough glucose has moved across in this way, the concentration will be lower in the lumen, and so the remaining glucose is absorbed in a different way to avoid wastage, through active transport with sodium ions – the energy required to do this is outweighed by that contained within the glucose. Firstly, sodium ions are actively transported out of epithelial cells into the blood, through a sodium potassium exchanger, and the lack of sodium this creates produces a concentration gradient, causing more sodium to diffuse into the cells from the lumen. They are forced to travel through a sodium-glucose co-transporter protein in the plasma membrane of the cell, however. This means that the diffusion brings in glucose, too, which can then travel along a concentration gradient into the blood by facilitated diffusion through a protein channel in the plasma membrane. This movement across membranes allows glucose to be taken into the body, and thus without it aerobic respiration could not occur. The adaptations of the membrane to allow this to happen are the folding on the intestinal side called microvilli, which produces a larger surface area and, therefore, increases absorption. The small intestine would not be able to function if not for its membrane.

Movement across the membrane also occurs in gaseous exchange, with oxygen and carbon dioxide crossing the membranes between the capillaries and alveoli in the lungs – oxygen into the deoxygenated blood and carbon dioxide out of it, along their respective concentration gradients. These gases, being small and uncharged, can pass straight through the membrane, allowing the excess carbon dioxide, which can dissociate into harmful carbonic acid, to be removed and the required oxygen added. A similar mechanism occurs in capillary beds in body tissue, with the reverse occurring once the now-oxygenated blood reaches tissues. Oxygen, which diffuses into the tissues is necessary as the terminal electron acceptor in aerobic respiration, and the carbon dioxide produced in respiration diffuses out and back into the blood. These two movements across membranes are necessary to both prevent carbonic acid from harming the body and to allow aerobic respiration – the exchange with the outside environment prolongs life.

Movement of substances across cell membranes is important for the process of transpiration, the movement of water up a plant. Firstly, water, along with mineral ions, is absorbed through root hair cells. After this, water travels through the root to the xylem, so it can travel to the leaf where it is needed. (There then continued a long extract about the passage of water through roots that is no longer needed).

A further example of movement across cell membranes can be seen within the nervous system, where different ions cross the membrane of neurone cells to prepare for and create action potentials. In order for resting potential to occur and be maintained at -70mV, potassium and sodium ions are constantly exchanged across the membrane of the neurone, with the former entering the cell and the latter leaving. As the potassium can then diffuse back out through potassium channels, whereas sodium channels are closed, there are more positively charged particles outside than inside creating a negative potential difference. When a stimulus is detected, some sodium channels are stimulated to open – pressure-mediated channels, for example, in the Pacinian corpuscle. This makes the potential less negative, as sodium can enter the neurone, and once the threshold of -55mV is reached, voltage-mediated sodium channels open, causing the potential to become positive and increase further – this is known as depolarisation. At +30mV, sodium channels are stimulated to close and potassium channels to open, causing repolarisation and, after a refractory period of hyperpolarisaton, returning the neurone to resting potential. Some sodium ions diffuse sideways during the initial depolarisation, stimulating an action potential further along the neurone – this wave of depolarisation is what allows electrical impulses to be transmitted along the neurone. The movement of particles across the membrane is what allows all of this, and so without this movement the nervous system would not function. Movement across membranes is necessary in synapses and between neurones too, where neurotransmitters are released from the presynaptic cleft in order to stimulate an action potential in the postsynaptic neurone: these are just yet more examples of this process's importance. Without this ability of animals to respond to their environment, they would not be able to survive.

As can been seen above, membranes are essential to all organisms. They are also essential to simpler bacteria as they act as their only barrier to the environment and fungi, which use extra-cellular digestion. It is likely that, for this reason, they were present in the formation of the first living organisms in evolution.

Other titles relate to membranes, although they are not specifically mentioned. A title from around 12 years ago was:

The process of osmosis and its importance to living organisms

The following aspects were demanded in the mark scheme, with the removal of water in plant roots. However, I don't see how there could be enough content to justify a similar title, but have included it for completeness.

1) Definition.
2) Effects on cells; turgidity and support; plasmolysis (idea); lysis; cystic fibrosis.
3) Importance of the role of animals in the relationship between plasma and tissue fluid; reabsorption in gut; sweat production neutral.
4) Importance of the role of plants in the movement of water from soil to leaves in plants; role in mass flow hypothesis for movement in plants.

A similar title and suggested content was:

The process of diffusion and its importance in living organisms.

1) The process itself is in AS/GCSE
2) Together with osmosis, as a special case of diffusion of water and how substances enter and leave cells
3) Gaseous exchange in lungs, gills and leaves
4) The uptake of the products of digestion
5) Exchange of material between blood in capillaries and tissue

6) The uptake of water by roots and root pressure, and in the mass flow hypothesis of the translocation of sugars

7) Regulation of blood water potential

8) Action potentials

9) Synaptic transmission

A subsequent title that could possibly lead on from here is the one below. I have, therefore, included an example essay for this one.

<u>The movement of substances within living organisms</u>

This year only four of the topics below were needed to access full marks. However, a good revision activity would be to see if you could sketch a paragraph on all of the sections. You can clearly see why the following essay was rewarded so highly. However, notice how simple its structure is and how it is more a series of coherent paragraphs

Again the content to include would be:

1) Plasma membranes and movement across

2) Protein synthesis

3) Movement through ER and Golgi

4) Cell division and chromosome movement

5) Water movement in plants/xylem

6) Translocation

7) Neurones and synaptic vesicles

8) Actin and myosin

9) DNA replication and mutation

10) Electron transport chains

11) Molecular/atomic/ionic movement

Many functions that cells carry out rely on substances entering and leaving the cell. Within the cell, substances also need to enter and leave certain organelles, such as the mitochondria. There are several processes by which substances can cross the membranes of the cell and organelles and I will explore them in this essay

The first and simplest process by which a substance can enter the cell is diffusion. This is when a substance moves from an area of high concentration to a lower concentration down a diffusion gradient. It is a passive process, and so no external energy input is required; only the kinetic energy of the particles. The process by which water moves across membranes is called osmosis and is defined as the movement of water molecules from an area of high water potential to low water potential across a partially permeable membrane. Of course, the water potential of pure water is 0, so all other water potentials are negative, with the higher the concentration of solutes, the more negative the water potential. In other words, water moves from a region with a negative water potential to a region with a more negative water potential. Again, this is a passive process, so no energy is required. Another mechanism of movement in and around cells is active transport. As the name would suggest, this is not a passive process and requires energy in the form of ATP in order to occur. Active transport is the movement of substances from an area of low concentration to an area of high concentration, and it relies on carrier proteins. The hydrolysis of ATP phosphorylates, the carrier protein, releases energy to transport hydrogen ions against its concentration gradient. When the hydrogen ions and the phosphate group bind to the trans membrane-carrier protein, it causes a change of shape, allowing a molecule (for example, glucose) to cross the membrane. When the phosphate group and hydrogen ion detach from the carrier protein, it will return to its original shape, ready to transport another molecule.

All substances that enter and leave the cell need to cross the plasma membrane, which consists of a phospholipid bilayer, as well as many embedded protein channels and carrier proteins. Small uncharged particles, as well as those that are lipid soluble, can diffuse directly through the phospholipid bilayer. However, charged particles (ions) and other large water soluble molecules rely on facilitated diffusion or active transport in order to cross the membrane. All ions cross the plasma membrane through protein channels, but it is important to note that each ion channel is specific to that ion and so other ions will not be able to use it to cross the membrane. Large molecules rely on carrier proteins in order to cross the membrane, but once again these are complementary to a specific molecule and so will not transport any other molecules across the membrane.

An example of how substances crossing the membrane of a cell are vital to the role of the cell would be in a neurone. When a neurone is at rest (with a potential difference across the membrane of -70mV) there are two processes occurring to maintain this potential difference.

Firstly, active transport: a sodium potassium pump transports 3 sodium ions out of the cell for every 2 potassium ions in. Also, the axon membrane is much more permeable to potassium ions than sodium ions, due to a relatively large number of open potassium ion channels; so potassium ions are also diffusing out of the axon more quickly than sodium is diffusing in. The maintenance of a resting potential is essential for effective nervous communication because it means that if a stimulus is applied (e.g. in the form of mechanical pressure) the neurone can send an action potential along and the brain can then coordinate a response. When a stimulus is applied, a generator potential is produced, and if this causes the membrane potential of the axon to reach threshold (-55mV), then the voltage gated sodium ion channels will open and there will be an influx of sodium ions into the axon, depolarising it. Once the membrane potential reaches +40mV, the voltage gated sodium ion channels close and the voltage gated potassium ion channels will open, so potassium ions will rush out of the axon, bringing the membrane potential down and depolarising the axon. However, the potassium ion channels are less sensitive than the sodium channels, so the membrane potential will fall below -70mV. This is called hyperpolarisaton or the refractory period. It is important that the refractory period occurs because it stops another action potential from being generated (because it is much less likely that threshold will be met) so the action potentials are kept discrete.

Movement also occurs in muscle cells when they are formed into fibres. Muscle contraction is essential in animals, as they need to move in order to stay alive: they need to find/gather food, escape from predators etc. When a muscle is stimulated and acetylcholine binds to its receptors to the surface of the muscle, the muscle becomes depolarised, as sodium ion channels open and sodium rushes in. This depolarisation causes calcium ions to be released from the sarcoplasmic reticulum and binds to its binding site on the troponin molecules. This causes a change of shape in the troponin, and as a result, the tropomyosin is moved and the actin filament is exposed. This allows the myosin head to bind to the binding site on the actin filament and ratchet the filament in during the power stroke. The detaching of the myosin head also requires energy from the hydrolysis of ATP by the enzyme ATPase. This movement of the actin filament towards the myosin causes the length of the sarcomere to shorten and, therefore, the animal is able to move.

Most of the genetic information of a cell is stored in the nucleus, in the form of DNA. DNA is associated with several proteins and does not leave the nucleus of the cell (which would increase the risk of corruption to the DNA, by mutation or digestion.) During the process of transcription, the sense strand of DNA is used as a template to create a complementary molecule of pre-messenger RNA. This is then spliced by removing the introns (non-coding sections.) The mRNA leaves the nucleus through a nuclear pore and joins with a ribosome, which is mostly found on the rough endoplasmic reticulum. The ribosome then 'reads' each of the codons on the mRNA and a tRNA molecule with the complementary anticodon (which is bonded to a specific amino acid) will bring the amino acid to the ribosome. As the ribosome moves along the mRNA, the sequence of amino acids is built up. They then join to each other via a peptide (amide) bond through a condensation reaction. Once the polypeptide has been completed (which occurs after the stop codon of the mRNA molecule), it is transported through the endoplasmic reticulum to the Golgi apparatus that prepares and 'packages' the protein. It is then stored in a vesicle until it is released from the cell.

In plants, osmosis plays a particularly vital role. As a result of open stomata, which allow the plants to exchange gases, a lot of water is lost by transpiration. This means that the water will need to be replaced. However, water is obtained through the roots of a plant, at the bottom, and the water is lost at the leaves, so it is transported through the xylem vessels. One way in which the plant does this is by generating a root pressure. Mineral ions are actively transported into the xylem vessels, which lowers the water potential, and so water will move by osmosis into the xylem. This pushes the water that is already in the xylem upwards. Another mechanism involved is cohesion-tension theory. This means that a negative pressure (i.e. tension) is generated by water moving by osmosis into the leaves. A tension is generated and so water is drawn up the xylem. One of the reasons this works is that there is cohesion between the water molecules: in other words, water is a polar molecule and can form relative strong hydrogen bonds. This means that the molecules 'stick' to each other as they are drawn up the xylem.

Overall, the movement of substances inside cells and mass flow transport throughout organisms is vital, as it allows reagent to enter the cell and waste products to be removed. Furthermore, movement of filaments inside cells, for example during muscle contraction or the contraction of microtubules for synaptic transmission, allows essential processes to occur.

ENZYMES

A common topic for essays is enzymes, as they are such a key component of biology; therefore, the A* essay below is a typical title. As always, make sure you answer the question that is asked, not the one you hope it is!

The part played by enzymes in the functioning of different cells, tissues and organs.

1) *Action of enzymes*
2) *Enzyme properties*
3) *Extracellular digestion*
4) *Nutrient cycles*
5) *Digestion in humans*
6) *Replication of DNA*
7) *Protein and enzyme synthesis*
8) *Metabolic pathways*
9) *Mutations*
10) *Coenzymes and enzyme action*
11) *Homeostasis*
12) *Neurone/synapse*
13) *Muscle contraction*
14) *Pesticide toxicity*

Remember, the title is 'the importance of enzymes', not – 'write about digestion and casually mention enzymes once in the paragraph'!

Enzymes are globular proteins that act as biological catalysts. They play a fundamental role in the control of chemical reactions, both inside and outside the cell. Without the ability of enzymes to make reactions occur, life would not be possible. In the essay below, I will summarise some the key reactions that occur and the importance of them.

Due to a specific sequence of amino acids in the enzyme's primary structure, the polymer will have a very specific tertiary structure/3D shape. Consequently, the active site is a very specific shape and will be complementary to only a single substrate. This means that it can only catalyse one type of reaction because it cannot form an enzyme-substrate complex with other molecules. A useful model to describe the action of enzymes is the lock and key model, which suggests that the active site of the enzyme is perfectly complementary to the shape of a substrate in the same way that a lock has the perfect shape for a specific key. Another model, called induced fit, suggests that the active site of the enzyme, although still specific to the substrate, changes shape slightly to allow it to become complementary as the binding occurs. This more recent theory is supported by x-ray crystallography images, which show the active site changing shape as the substrate binds.

Perhaps the most obvious role played by enzymes would be the role they play in digestion. In this process, large molecules are broken down into their individual respective monomers and this relies (for the most part) on different enzymes to catalyse the hydrolysis reactions. For example, starch is broken down into glucose by these enzymes. Firstly, amylase will hydrolyse the α-1,4-glycosidic bonds to form many molecules of maltose. The disaccharide maltose will then be hydrolysed by the enzyme maltase which, again, breaks the glycosidic bond between the molecules in a hydrolysis reaction, and two molecules of glucose are formed. As they are now small and soluble they are able to be absorbed into the blood via the small intestine. This is an essential process as the glucose which is produced has a variety of uses including acting as the respiratory substrate for aerobic (and anaerobic) respiration.

The two most important biochemical processes that occur in any ecosystem are photosynthesis and respiration. Both of these involve enzymes (and coenzymes) at every stage. In the light dependent stage of photosynthesis, enzymes are involved in each step, most notably in the generation of ATP by photophosphorylation with the enzyme ATPase (ATPsynthase) by chemiosmosis. Furthermore, one of the main products of the light dependent reaction is the reduced coenzyme NADPH. It is also important to note that many of the enzymes involved in this stage are embedded into the membrane of the thylakoid. Conversely, the enzymes involved in the Calvin cycle are found in the stroma of the chloroplast. In the first stage of the light independent reaction, atmospheric carbon is fixated by a 5 carbon intermediate, ribulose bisphosphate, and this fixation uses the enzyme rubisco (ribulose bisphosphate carboxylase.) This will produce two molecules of glycerate-3-phosphate, which is then reduced to triose phosphate by the reduced NADP and energy from ATP. TP can then be converted into useful organic substances, such as glucose. However, the enzyme rubisco is also involved in photorespiration. In this, Rubisco catalyses a reaction between RuBP and atmospheric oxygen. As a result, less glycerate-3-phosphate is formed (because phosphoglycolate is also formed) and so the efficiency of photosynthesis falls, as fewer molecules of RuBP are regenerated.

Enzymes are also involved in some of the most important processes that occur in the cell: DNA replication, transcription and translation (the central dogma of molecular biology.) During DNA replication, which is semi- conservative, the enzyme DNA helicase 'unzips' the double helix of DNA by breaking the hydrogen bonds between complementary base pairs. Free floating nucleotides then form hydrogen bonds with the now exposed bases of the DNA strand. Another enzyme, DNA polymerase, joins together the free-floating nucleotides by forming phosphodiester bonds between them, and forming new strands of DNA. Similarly, during transcription, a molecule of pre-mRNA is formed when the enzyme RNA polymerase joins free floating RNA nucleotides together. During translation, an enzyme called aminoacyl tRNA synthetase joins an amino acid to a tRNA molecule, which will then go to a ribosome for translation. All of these genetic processes rely heavily on specific enzymes and the processes are essential, as they produce proteins, some of which may be involved in fundamental life processes, for example, in respiration. Some other peptides produced include hormones, such as insulin, which is involved in homeostasis – specifically the control of blood glucose concentration.

In animals, an important use of ATP is for muscle contraction, as this allows movement for escaping predators, chasing prey and many others. When a muscle is stimulated, the neurotransmitter binds to receptors on the membrane of the muscle tissue, and the T tubules allow the muscle tissue to all be stimulated almost simultaneously. The depolarisation of the muscle tissue, caused by the opening of voltage gated sodium ion channels, causes the sarcoplasmic reticulum to release calcium ions. These bind to troponin, causing a change of shape and, subsequently, the tropomyosin molecule is pulled away and the binding site on the actin molecule is exposed. The myosin head binds to the actin and pulls it. In order for the myosin head to detach from the actin, energy from ATP is needed and the enzyme ATPase hydrolyses the ATP molecule into ADP and Pi in order to provide this energy. This clearly demonstrates the fundamental role played by enzymes in muscle contraction.

In conclusion, enzymes control almost all biochemical reactions and play as important a role in single celled organisms as they do in complex multicellular organisms, such as human beings (*homo sapiens*). As previously mentioned, the reactions they catalyse are essential in the functioning of many cells and, consequently, the survival of the organism.

Condensation and hydrolysis and their importance in biology

This is quite a vague title and one that I would avoid. However, below, is an essay based on the mark scheme.

1) Synthesis of proteins, carbohydrates and lipids from monomers
2) Large molecules are important in the structure and functioning of cells
3) Hydrolysis of proteins, carbohydrates and lipids from monomers
4) Large molecules are important in the structure and functioning of cells
5) Digestion of food
6) Digestion of cellulose
7) DNA, RNA and protein synthesis
8) The role of ATP

The ability to build up and break down molecules is essential in any living organism. As a result, there are many examples of condensation and hydrolysis reactions respectively. In the essay below, I have outlined a few examples and stressed their importance to the living organism.

The most common condensation reactions are in the formation of polymers. For example, glycosidic bonds in carbohydrates. At the earliest stage two α-glucose molecules bond together to form maltose. In this, the hydroxide groups at carbon 1 of one glucose and 4 of the other react. Water is formed (hence a condensation reaction) and the remaining oxygen atom form an ester bond between the two. This can then be repeated between subsequent maltose molecules to form starch and glycogen. This is important as it means the soluble energy source can be made into insoluble polymers, making storage possible as there will be no osmotic effect. A similar reaction happens in the primary structure of proteins with the formation of peptide bonds between the amino group of one amino acid and the carboxylic acid of another. A condensation reaction is also needed to convert glycerol and fatty acids and/or phosphate into triglyceride/phospholipids. Without these macromolecules organisms couldn't form membranes or enzymes, so therefore life could not exist.

In a similar way, organisms must be able to break down these macromolecules to be able to absorb them. These breaking down reactions are hydrolysis. The specific nature of a hydrolysis reaction is that the addition of water (hydro) is needed to break the bond (lysis), in effect the reverse of a condensation reaction. The most obvious example of this is digestion where enzymes catalyse the hydrolysis of large insoluble molecules to their constituent soluble molecules, so that they can pass through membranes. Starch in plants is hydrolysed to maltose by amylase in the saliva, which in turn is hydrolysed to maltose in the small intestine allowing it to be absorbed. Proteins are hydrolysed by proteases in the stomach and small intestine and fats by lipases after being emulsified by bile. One of the few molecules that can't be hydrolysed by mammals is cellulose in the cell wall of plants. It, therefore, makes up the fibre of food. Some bacteria are able to digest this, however, as they have evolved to produce enzymes that they can excrete extra-cellularly. These hydrolyse the β-1,4-glycosdic bond between the β-glucose molecules making the sugar smaller and soluble. It can, therefore, be absorbed into the bacteria. These bacteria can form mutualistic relationships in the guts of ruminant animals.

The ability of condensation reactions to make stable polymers is again exploited in genetics. DNA and RNA are polymers of nucleotides. The nucleotides consist of a nitrogenous base, a phosphate group and deoxyribose and ribose sugars respectively. The sequence of these nucleotides, is specifically what enables the genetic code to work. If just one nucleotide is in the wrong mutation, this can cause a disease like cystic fibrosis. The phosphodiester bonds between the sugar of one nucleotide and the phosphate of another is very stable and makes sure that they stay in the right order. Enzymes are able to hydrolyse this. An example would be the restriction endonucleases that are naturally occurring in prokaryotes. They are able to hydrolyse at specific base sequences of double stranded DNA. This ability to specifically hydrolyse DNA is used in genetic engineering so that specific genes and sections of DNA can be an hydrolysed form of chromosomes. A second type of enzyme, DNA ligase, is then able to join the complementary staggered ends back together in with a condensation reaction. These are, therefore, very important reactions in biotechnology.

A final important example of condensation and hydrolytic reactions is the transfer of energy to and from ATP. When ATP is formed from ADP and P_i in a condensation reaction, the energy from this comes from the flow of protons from an intermembrane space through ATP synthetase. In the case of the light dependent reactions of photosynthesis this is essential to transfer the light energy into chemical energy within this terminal bond. This energy is then released when the bond is hydrolysed. A good example is in the sliding filament theory of muscle contraction. Here, the hydrolysis of the ATP causes the myosin head to move and overlap the actin. This is what causes movement. The hydrolysis of ATP also enables active transport to happen and therefore move essential ions, so as those in roots from the soil or glucose in the small intestine across a membrane.

As can be seen above, many reactions are either hydrolysis (catabolic) or condensation (anabolic) and are fundamental to the survival of an organism. Whether it be the building or breakdown of complex molecules or the facilitation of reactions, which allow instant movement in response to danger, these reactions are vital for survival.

A related title would be looking at energy transfers within an organism and below is an essay that fits this bill. Be careful to not confuse this with energy transfer between organisms, which is an ecology title.

Energy transfers that take place in living organisms

1) ATP synthesis from ADP and P; role as an energy source

2) Photosynthesis: excitation of electrons; generation of ATP and reduced NADP; Photolysis; reduction of glycerate phosphate to carbohydrate; structure of chloroplast in relation to energy transfers

3) Respiration; net gain of ATP in glycolysis; production of ATP in Krebs cycle; synthesis of ATP associated with electron transfer chain; ATP production in anaerobic respiration; structure of mitochondrion in relation to energy transfers
4) Uses of energy in biological processes: active transport; muscle contraction; nerve transmission; synthesis; translocation; nitrogen fixation; receptors.

Energy transfers are necessary in living organisms in order to preserve life, for all essential life processes require energy in different forms and places. ATP is used as the biological currency of energy, and so energy transfers can be seen in its production and use throughout the body.

ATP itself is synthesised by adding a third inorganic phosphate group to ADP and it is the breakdown of this bond by ATPase which releases energy, and makes ATP useful as a molecule. The fact that this is a simple, one-step reaction is particularly advantageous. ATP, too, is both small and soluble and cannot be transported between cells, making it perfect for providing a local source of energy, after being produced through respiration by ATP synthase.

The production of ATP, through the process of respiration, is one example of an energy transfer in living organisms. Energy is ultimately transferred from molecules of glucose to the bond between ADP and a third phosphate group, through the formation of ATP, but this occurs in several stages. Initially, glucose is broken down into two molecules of pyruvate in glycolysis, which requires some energy from ATP but also produces some ATP, leading to a net gain of two molecules of ATP per molecule of glucose, which is all that can be produced in anaerobic respiration. In aerobic respiration, pyruvate is turned into acetyl-CoA in the link reaction. It is then used to convert oxaloacetate into citrate, which slowly turns back into oxaloacetate in the Krebs cycle. All of these processes involve energy transfers in the conversion of molecules into other molecules and release various other substances in the process, including most importantly NADH and FADH. This is how the primary energy transfer of respiration occurs – these NADH and FADH molecules are converted into NAD and FAD in the process of oxidative respiration. The electrons released go along the electron transport chain, providing energy that is used to pump the protons released across the inner membrane of the mitochondria, against their concentration gradient. They then diffuse back along this gradient through ATP synthase, producing ATP, before combining with electrons and oxygen – the terminal electron acceptor – to make water. This entire process involves various energy transfers, for energy must be provided to ADP to form ATP.

But this glucose must itself be produced, which occurs through photosynthesis. This is another example of an energy transfer in living organisms, for this process relies on light energy (entering from outside the plant) to produce chemical energy in the form of glucose, with this light energy acting to excite electrons, raising them into a higher energy state in order to actively pump protons against a proton gradient – these protons then diffuse back across the gradient through ATP synthase, forming ATP. The electrons, on the other hand, are excited again by light energy and combine with NADP to reduce it, forming NADPH. NADPH and ATP are then used in the Calvin cycle to fix carbon, but in order for this to occur, they must have been formed, which relies on these energy transfers.

ATP is then used up in a variety of ways, all of which are, once again, examples of energy transfer, as this is the purpose of ATP. In active transport, for example, energy is required to move molecules against their concentration gradient (normally, they would go the opposite direction through diffusion), and so is transferred from the molecule ATP, which becomes ADP in the process, releasing an inorganic phosphate molecule. This energy can, for example, be required to make a carrier protein change shape, moving a molecule from one side of a membrane to another. An example of the importance of active transport is in neurones, where it is required to maintain a negative resting potential, through actively exchanging potassium and sodium, the former into the neurone, although it is then allowed to diffuse back out, and the latter out, creating more positive charges outside than in – a negative potential difference. This requires the energy transfer in the conversion of ATP to ADP in order to take place.

ATP is also required for muscle contraction, providing the energy for the myosin head to pull on the actin filaments, causing both actin and myosin filaments to move closer together and thus contracting the whole muscle. After calcium ions have been released onto the muscle, stimulating it to contract by attaching to troponin, moving tropomyosin out of the way of the actin-myosin binding site and, therefore, allowing the myosin head to attach to the actin filament, ATP is converted into ADP, releasing energy which allows the myosin head to pull the actin filament along, before detaching and moving back into shape, which requires more ATP. This energy transfer, therefore, is crucial in allowing, for example, the movement of many organisms.

So, as can be clearly seen above, it is essential for energy to be transferred within an organism. The movement from chemical to kinetic energy or vice versa allows the essential life processes to occur.

Cells are easy to distinguish by their shape. How are the shapes of cells related to their functions?

You can see from the suggested content below that there are many angles you could take here:

1) Epithelial cells - intestinal, alveolar, gill lamellae: Two examples allowed as appropriate, relating to transport function(s):
(collectively) large SA: flattened – short diffusion pathway; folded membrane larger SA for stated function
2) Blood – transport: red blood cells; biconcave shape – increase SA for oxygen exchange; move through capillaries
3) Blood – exchange: endothelial cells of capillaries; flattened – short diffusion pathway
4) Blood – white cells: phagocytes/macrophages; amoeboid properties; related to movement into tissues/engulfing e.g. bacteria
5) Nervous system – neurones (and Schwann cells): dendrites – make synaptic connection to other neurones; axon/dendron – carry nerve impulses over long distances; shapes of relay, motor and sensory; related to function; myelin sheath – faster transmission of impulses
6) Nervous system – receptors – NB could be other than light: cone/rod cells with distinctive 'heads' – containing pigment; detect light; dendrites to synapse with bipolar/ganglion cell(s)
7) Muscle: elongated – contain rows of sarcomeres: leads to contraction in length; force generated in particular plane; branched in cardiac – gives contraction in more than one plane
8) Ciliated: cells lining air passages/oviducts; push mucus/eggs along; remove trapped microorganisms/towards uterus

Most cells carry out different functions. A group of identical cells that carry out a similar function is called a tissue, and tissues that work together to carry out a process constitute an organ. Each cell is specialised to carry out its function and a large part of its adaptations relate to the shape of the cell itself.

Within plants, an example of how the shapes of certain cells are related to their function would be the palisade cells in the upper mesophyll layer of the leaf. They are arranged vertically, rather than horizontally, which means that more cells can be packed into the upper layer of the leaf. The advantage of this arrangement is that it increases the exposure of the chloroplasts (and thus the chlorophyll pigments) to sunlight. This means that the light dependent reaction will occur more quickly and reduced NADP and ATP will be produced at a faster rate. Therefore, the Calvin cycle will occur more quickly, as glycerate-3-phosphate will be reduced to triose phosphate. The triose phosphate can then either be used to produce glucose or other useful organic compounds, or can be used to regenerate the 5-carbon intermediate, ribulose bisphosphate. In reality, one-sixth of the TP is used to produce useful organic compounds and the remaining five-sixths is used to regenerate RuBP. Furthermore, the long palisade cells have certain adaptations to ensure that the chloroplasts do not get damaged. For instance, if there is a risk of sunlight damaging the chloroplasts, the microtubules in the palisade cell will contract and drag the chloroplasts towards the bottom of the cell, thereby reducing the risk of damage.

Animals also have many different types of cells whose structures relate strongly to their functions. An example of such a cell would be the epithelial cells in the small intestine. These have finger-shaped extensions called microvilli which increase the surface area of the cell, thereby allowing a faster rate of diffusion. In addition, there are many embedded proteins in the plasma membrane of the epithelial cells. These allow processes, such as facilitated diffusion and active transport, to occur more quickly and the cell to achieve its vital role of absorbing nutrients. In a similar way, cells that are adapted for gas exchange have similar adaptations. The cells on the surface of the alveoli and the lamellae of gills are adapted to maximise the gas exchange across their membranes. They are thin, so that the diffusion pathway is short.

Once the oxygen has entered the bloodstream, it binds to a haemoglobin molecule within a red blood cell. With the absence of a nucleus, the cells are able to form a biconcave shape. This means that they are able to have a large surface area to volume ratio. As such, it is more likely that the oxygen will come into contact with the haemoglobin and bind. As the red blood cells are relatively small they are able to fit through the small capillaries and access all areas of the circulatory system.

A further example of a type of cell whose shape is related to its function is the muscle cell or fibre. The elongated fibres that share nuclei have a very specific structure, which is closely related to its function. Firstly, at the neuromuscular junction, the membrane of the muscle contains extensions/folds called T-tubules. These allow the neurotransmitter (acetylcholine) to travel deep into the muscle fibres and stimulate the entire muscle to contract almost simultaneously. Furthermore, the sarcomeres (contractile unit) of each myofibril are staggered and arranged linearly. In terms of the filaments themselves, it is the shape of the myosin that allows the muscle contraction to occur, and due to their shape, they contract along their longitudinal axis. This means they contract in a predictable way causing the attached bones to move. An exception to this is cardiac muscle, which is branched so that it contracts in three dimensions. This branched shape helps it achieve its role of making the heart contract in such a way that it can pump blood around the body.

The neurones that make up the nervous system also have highly specialised cells with specific shapes. Firstly, the ends of neurones have long extensions called dendrites, which make connections with other neurones and can receive action potentials. Neurones also have a long, thin axon which the sodium ions can rapidly diffuse down when there is an action potential. Also, the presence of Schwann cells forms the myelin sheath, which speeds up the rate that the action potential travels along the axon. The cells wrap around the axon and act as insulators, so that no sodium or potassium can enter/leave the axon at these points. Instead, the depolarisation occurs at the gaps between the Schwann cells, called the nodes of

Ranvier. In effect, this means that the action potential 'jumps' from node to node by saltatory conduction, and this is much faster than it would be in an unmyelinated neurone.

Overall, there are many cells that rely on their specific shape to carry out a function. The process by which they obtain this shape is called differentiation and if a cell is damaged and loses its specific shape, it is likely the cell will die. Whether it has a role in communication such as dendrites or absorption as those of the small intestine specialisation and adaption over evolution have found solutions over time.

ECOLOGY

As I said at the beginning, almost every year there is an essay with a biochemistry theme. That is why they have taken up over half of the book! Titles, however, can come from a range of other angles. In this chapter, I have collated a number of those that come from Ecology. As before, this is only the stem and, like in any good essay you need to include knowledge from all parts of the specification. As you will see, they mostly derive from the ecological cycles, but I have included any others here as well. You may, like I do, reflect that some of these A/A* essays are shorter and not as well constructed. I put this down to the fact that so few candidates attempt these titles that the bar is lower to get the top grades. However, AQA would dispute this and, therefore, feel free to read into this what you will.

One thing to realise is that although the title of the essay below seems to relate to the nitrogen cycle you can, and should, look beyond this, and from marking point 3 onwards, it has a lot of parts that you would find in a biochemistry essay. The main learning point here is you give yourself the time to mull over the title as you do the rest of the paper. I have spoken to many candidates who only finally clicked what topics could be included in an essay with 5 minutes to go, and by then it was too late.

How nitrogen-containing substances are made available to and are used by living organisms

1) *Nitrogen cycle*
2) *The influence of deforestation of nitrogen cycling*
3) *Proteins as biological molecules*
4) *Enzymes and enzyme action*
5) *Haemoglobin and the exchange of respiratory gases*
6) *The use of membrane proteins in the nervous system*
7) *DNA and protein synthesis*
8) *Chlorophyll, NADP and photosynthesis*
9) *ATP and respiration*

Nitrogen is a key element in living organisms, as it is used to produce several key molecules. For example, there is a nitrogen atom in the amine group of amino acids and there is nitrogen present in the nitrogenous bases (thymine, uracil, adenine, cytosine and guanine), which make up DNA and RNA. Therefore, it is important that living organisms can obtain a sufficient amount of nitrogen in order to produce these compounds.

The nitrogen cycle best describes the ways in which nitrogen containing compounds are made available to living organisms. When an organism dies, its dead matter, which contains nitrogen, is released into the soil. Here, saprobiotic bacteria release enzymes into the soil to hydrolyse the dead plant or animal matter by extra cellular digestion, and one of the products of this process is ammonium ions – this process is called ammonification. Ammonium ions can then be oxidised in a process called nitrification by nitrifying bacteria that converts the ammonium ions, first into nitrite ions (or nitrate iii) and then into nitrate ions (v). These nitrate ions can then be actively transported into the plant through the roots and used for producing proteins and other compounds. When an animal consumes a plant, a lot of the nitrogen containing compounds are hydrolysed by enzymes. For example, the proteins are hydrolysed by protease enzymes, which break the peptide (amide) bonds between the amino acids. The amino acids can then be absorbed by the epithelial cells of the small intestine and enter the bloodstream, where they will be transported to different regions of the body and used to produce proteins. Of course, if an animal or plant dies, its nitrogen containing compounds are returned to the soil, where they will be hydrolysed by saprobionts and the cycle repeats itself. Another aspect of the nitrogen cycle is the role played by nitrogen fixing bacteria. Nitrogen fixing bacteria, which exist either in the soil (free-living) or in the root nodules of leguminous plants (mutualistic), convert atmospheric nitrogen into ammonium ions in a process called nitrogen fixation. The bacteria which live in the root nodules of plants have a symbiotic relationship with the plants. Once the ammonium ions have been produced, they can be converted into nitrates by nitrifying bacteria.

Perhaps the most important nitrogen containing compounds are proteins, as these have innumerable functions within living organisms. Amino acids can form a peptide (or amide) bond by reacting the carboxyl group of one acid to the amine group of an adjacent acid. Once lots of amino acids have been joined together, a polypeptide is formed. The amino acids within the polypeptide then interact with each other by forming hydrogen bonds, ionic bonds and disulphide bonds, if the amino acid cysteine is present. This causes the polypeptide to fold up to a have a very specific 3D shape, and this shape (i.e. the tertiary structure of the protein) is very closely related to the function of the protein. One example of the importance of the shape is demonstrated by enzymes. Enzymes have a very specifically shaped active site, which is complementary to the shape of one type of substrate. This allows the enzyme to act as a biological catalyst, for one type of reaction, because it can form an enzyme-substrate complex and catalyse the reaction by providing an alternative mechanism (which is also likely to have a lower activation energy.) If, however, something causes the enzyme to lose its shape, for example, by heating the enzyme and breaking the hydrogen bonds in its tertiary structure, the enzyme loses its ability to catalyse reactions, as fewer enzyme-substrate complexes can be formed.

Often, many proteins are made up of more than one polypeptide, and the way in which the different polypeptides interact in the protein is described as the quaternary structure. One such protein, which is made up of 4 polypeptide chains, is haemoglobin, which is responsible for transporting oxygen around the body. Each of the globular polypeptides contains a haem, and this contains an iron atom that bonds to the oxygen, reversibly, when there is a relatively high partial pressure of oxygen. If there is then a fall in the partial pressure of oxygen, which would be the case in respiring cells, the oxygen will dissociate from the haemoglobin, so that it could be used as the terminal electron acceptor for aerobic respiration.

Overall, proteins have many uses and are involved in other essential functions, for example antibodies are absolutely vital in order to have immunity. There are also fibrous proteins, such as collagen, which may be used for structural support.

Almost all of a cell's genetic information is stored in the nucleus of the cell, in the form of DNA. DNA exists as a double helix and each strand of DNA is made up of individual nucleotides that are bonded together by phosphodiester bonds. The two strands are held together by hydrogen bonds between the complementary base pairs. One of the main elements that makes up the bases in DNA (and RNA) is nitrogen; hence, they are often referred to as nitrogenous bases. One of the main functions of DNA is to replicate, because when a cell replicates, each of the daughter cells needs a copy of the DNA. During DNA replication, which occurs during the interphase of the cell cycle, the enzyme DNA helicase 'unzips' the double helix by breaking the hydrogen bonds between the complementary base pairs. Each strand is now exposed and can act as a template for free floating DNA nucleotides to bond to by hydrogen bonds. When the complementary base pairs have been made, the enzyme DNA polymerase joins together the free-floating nucleotides to form another strand of DNA. The reason that semi-conservative replication is advantageous is that it reduces the risk of mutations because the DNA already present acts as a template. As previously mentioned, once the DNA has been replicated, the cell can then divide by mitosis. The cell division allows for growth and repair of certain tissues and organs, as the new daughter cells can replace those that have been damaged or corrupted.

The main function of DNA, however, is to retain the genetic information of the cell, so that it can be used for protein synthesis – which is done through transcription and translation. Firstly, a transcription factor will bind to a promoter region of DNA and this will stimulate RNA polymerase. As the transcription factor complex moves along the DNA, it breaks the complementary base pairings by breaking the hydrogen bonds. The exposed sense strand of the DNA then acts as a template for free floating RNA nucleotides to bond to and RNA polymerase will join the RNA nucleotides together to form a molecule of pre-messenger RNA. Once the DNA has been transcribed, the sense and antisense strands of DNA will then reform their hydrogen bonds. Before the pre-mRNA can be translated to form a polypeptide, the non-coding sections (introns) must be removed by a process called splicing. Once spliced, the mRNA leaves the nucleus through a nuclear pore and travels through the cytoplasm to join with a ribosome. The ribosome will proceed to 'read' each codon and a molecule of transfer-RNA that bears the correct, complementary anticodon will come to the ribosome. Each of the tRNA molecules is carrying a specific amino acid. In this way, as the ribosome moves along the mRNA molecule, the primary structure of the polypeptide is produced. Once the ribosome reaches the 'stop' codon, the polypeptide will be completed. It is then transported along the rough endoplasmic reticulum to the Golgi apparatus, where it will fold up into a specific 3D shape by forming hydrogen, ionic and disulphide bonds. The completed protein will then be stored in a vesicle, until it is transported out of the cell.

Overall, nitrogen is an extremely important element and the recycling of nitrogen is what allows ecosystems to flourish. Its presence in biological molecules, such as amino acids and the bases of nucleotides, makes it an invaluable resource that organisms would not be able to live without.

Similar previous titles and topics you might consider are below. There is an essay for the second one.

Describe how nitrogen-containing substances are taken into, and metabolised in, animals and plants

1) Active transport and facilitated diffusion

2) Biological molecules, carbohydrates and proteins

3) Digestion and absorption of the products

4) Replication of DNA, protein synthesis

5) Digestion of cellulose

6) Method of removing nitrogenous wastes. Deamination and the production of urea

Again, a more general title below is cycles in biology, which could be biochemistry, physiology or ecology. From the topics to include notes, you will see that it could have fitted into a number of areas in this book. However, I have added it here as I feel it links a range of areas together. As stated before, an excellent essay does not have to include all of the mark points, just 4 or 5 covered in good depth.

Cycles in Biology

1) Nitrogen cycle: the role of microorganisms in the processes of saprophytic nutrition, deamination, nitrification, nitrogen fixation and denitrification. (Names of individual species are not required.)

2) Krebs cycle: acetylcoenzyme A combines with a four-carbon molecule to produce a six-carbon molecule that enters Kreb's cycle; the four carbon compound is regenerated during a cycle involving a series of oxidation reactions and the release of carbon dioxide; production of ATP and reduced NAD and FAD.

3) Electron transport chain: cyclical reduction and oxidation of NAD, FAD and other 'carriers'.

4) Synthesis and breakdown of ATP.

5) Light-independent reactions – Carbon dioxide accepted by RuBP to form two molecules of glycerate-3-phosphate, reduction of glycerate-3-phosphate to carbohydrate, and regeneration of RuBP.

6) Negative feedback mechanisms: Regulation of body temperature / blood glucose/blood water potential.

7) Cardiac cycle: relate pressure and volume changes in the heart and aorta to the maintenance of blood flow.

8) The role of tropomyosin, calcium ions and ATP in the cycle of actomyosin bridge formation.

9) Nerve function – depolarisation/repolarisation of a neurone in terms of differential membrane permeability and Na/K pumps, synthesis and re-synthesis of acetylcholine (synaptic transmission)/rhodopsin (rods) and restoration of a resting potential.

10) Mitosis/cell cycle – explanation of stages of mitosis, importance in growth and asexual reproduction.

11) Meiosis – importance in maintaining constant chromosome number from generation to generation; outline of the process (details of stages not required).

12) Examples of life cycles might be provided in terms of mitosis, meiosis, fertilisation and chromosome number.

13) DNA replication – semi-conservative.

Cycles are an essential part of biology. Their importance to organisms is both on a cellular level of the cell cycle but also on a wider eco-system level, which includes the recycling of compounds in the carbon and nitrogen cycles.

Mitosis of cells is required for the growth of any organism, but is also useful for the replacement of dead and damaged tissue. Mitosis can be understood in 5 different stages. The first stage being interphase where DNA replication and organelle replication occurs. The next stage is prophase, which is where the chromatin condenses to form chromosomes and the centrioles move to opposite poles of the cell. In metaphase, the centrioles spinning spindle fibres now bound to the centromere of the chromosome align the chromosomes at the equator of the cell. The next stage is anaphase, where spindle fibres contract and pull the sister chromatids to opposite poles of the cell. The last stage is telophase, where the cytoplasm divides into 2 via the process of cytokinesis, thus dividing the cell into 2.

The cardiac cycle is the process by which blood in humans is oxygenated and transported around the body. This is achieved by means of a double circulatory system and the use of a heart made up of myogenic cells for a pump. Blood from the right ventricle upon ventricular systole is transported to the lungs via the pulmonary artery, out of the semi-lunar valves. Here the deoxygenated blood is oxygenated and transported back to the left atrium of the heart by the pulmonary vein. This then moves into the left ventricle through the bicuspid pressure based valves in atrial systole. Upon ventricular systole, blood from the left ventricle is transported via the aorta around the whole body. The aorta branches off into arterioles and then into capillaries, thus reaching tissue fluid bathing cells all over the body. The blood is carried from the capillaries back into the heart via veins through the help of skeletal muscle contraction and pocket valves. Finally, the blood is returned to the heart in the right atrium by the superior and inferior vena cava.

In both respiration and photosynthesis, the electron transport chain is in action. Reducing agents are cycled in and out as they donate their electrons to the cytochromes. These are essential in the formation of the proton gradient, which causes the condensation reaction between ADP and P_i by ATP synthetase. When oxidised the NAD/FAD, in the case of respiration, or NADP, in the case of the light dependent reactions, return to be reduced again and as such recycled.

The Krebs cycle is an essential in respiration as it reduces 3 coenzymes of NAD and 1 FAD coenzyme per cycle. These are a quintessential part of oxidative phosphorylation and thus the production of ATP. The acetyl CoA combines with oxaloacetate to form a 6 carbon compound of citrate. The citrate is then oxidised back to oxaloacetate by the NAD and FAD, which in turn are reduced. Two decarboxylations also take place and a molecule of ATP is produced through substrate level phosphorylation.

The control contraction of muscles can also be seen as a cycle. The tropomyosin molecule prevents the myosin head from attaching to the binding site of the actin molecule. This makes sure that contraction is regulated and only occurs when an action potential arrives at the fibre. An action potential causes calcium to be released from the endoplasmic reticulum that binds to the tropomyosin. This causes a conformational change in the shape of the tropomyosin and so the myosin binding sites on the actin molecule are exposed. The myosin heads are now able to bind and with the hydrolysis of ATP to ADP by ATPase cause the movement of the myosin head. As many of these heads move together so the actin and myosin filaments slide over each other and the sarcomere contracts. The cyclical dissociation and rebinding of new ATP molecules and their subsequent hydrolysis means contraction continues.

Nitrogen is recycled in the eco-system through the nitrogen cycle. When plants and animals die they are decomposed by detritivores via a process called holozoic nutrition. This increases the surface of the organic matter for the action of saprobionts. The saprobionts release extra-cellular enzymes, which digest the protein containing nitrogen via hydrolysis into amino acids and are the deaminated into ammonium ions. Nitrifying bacteria, such as *Nitrozomas*, oxidise the ammonium ions into nitrites and *Nitrobacter* then oxidises these into nitrates. The nitrates are then actively transported into the root hair cell of plants to be used for the production of amino acids, DNA and RNA, thus completing the cycle.

PCR is a man-made technological cycle used in genetics. It stands for Polymerase Chain Reaction. A thermo-cycler is used to amplify a sample fragment of DNA. The hydrogen bonds in the DNA are separated by heating the sample up to 95^C. The separated DNA are then cooled to 55°C, which allows the primers to anneal by complementary base pairs to the ends of the DNA strands. The temperature is then heated to 92°C, which is the optimum temperature for the thermally stable *Taq* polymerase (a type of DNA polymerase that does not denature at high temperatures). It joins the sugar-phosphate backbone and attaches the complementary DNA nucleotides thereby replicating the strand. The process is repeated and each time the DNA sample is doubled via replication.

In conclusion, cycles are a fundamental aspect of both biological functions within organisms but also the future of biological technology. They can be influenced and controlled by human interactions, such as in the cases of fertilisers and the pill; however, many are essential for life to continue.

There are many different types of relationships and interactions between organisms

All organisms are interrelated and largely dependent on other organisms. Some organisms are essential for others to survive, for example, they are part of nutrient cycles or are in mutualistic relationships. Other organisms may interact by causing disease, for example, the relationship between pathogens and humans.

A prime example of a group of independent organisms are the carbon and nitrogen cycles. Saprobionts are micro-organisms which are essential for releasing CO_2 from dead organic matter back into the atmosphere. This is then absorbed through the stomata of plants for photosynthesis. They also release ammonium ions into the soil from nitrogen containing compounds in the dead organic matter, for example DNA or amino acids. The saprobionts achieve this by extra-cellular digestion. They release various hydrolytic enzymes that catalyse the breakdown of larger organic matter into smaller soluble compounds. These are then absorbed into the microorganisms and incorporated into their own macro-molecules. The ammonium ions in the soil are then oxidised by nitrifying bacteria, for example, *Nitrobacter* or *Nitrosomas*, which oxidise the ammonium ions into nitrates that can be absorbed by the root hair cells of plants by active transport. The plants are then able to use this nitrogen in the assimilation of amino acids to make proteins and nitrogenous bases in DNA and RNA.

Many organisms are involved in mutualistic symbiotic relationships. For example, between the bacteria *Rhizobium*, which is a class of nitrogen fixing bacteria that forms a symbiotic relationship within legumes. This allows both organisms to survive in areas where nitrogen content in the soil is low. The *Rhizobium* is able to convert nitrogen gas from the atmosphere into ammonium ions, which can be used by plants to create amino acids and DNA, and in return receives glucose as a respiratory substrate for respiration.

Other organisms may be pathogens, and thus cause disease in humans. For example, *Vibrio choleroe* is an example of a bacterial pathogen that can cause disease in humans. It affects the small intestine of sufferers by releasing proteins that are able to bind to various glycoprotein receptors and cause the chloride ion channels to open. The chloride ions move out of the epithelial cells in the lumen of the small intestine, where it lowers the water potential. Water then moves out of the epithelial cells via osmosis into the lumen, causing dehydration and diarrhoea.

However, not all bacteria cause disease in humans. Some bacteria, such as commensal organisms, are involved in the first line of defence in preventing pathogens from causing disease in humans. These organisms are bacteria that live on the surface of the skin and use the nutrients available, thus increasing competition for a potential pathogen. This intraspecific competition reduces the population of pathogenic bacterium on the skin, thus reducing the likelihood of disease upon the formation of a small cut.

Succession is another example of where organisms are inter-related and change the ecosystem over a period of time until a dynamic equilibrium of a climax community is reached. Pioneer species initially colonise an area of bare rock. A typical example of a pioneer is lichen. This is another example of a mutualistic relationship, but this time the fungus and algae involved co-exist. The algae photosynthesises to produce glucose, which the fungus benefits from, and in exchange, the fungus converts some to nitrates that the algae can use. Without this positive interaction, it would not be possible for either organism to survive. As they die and the abiotic conditions become less hostile, so other xerophytes and moss start to colonise. These then survive and reproduce, and when they die they are decomposed by microorganisms that convert humus into a thin layer of bare soil with some available nutrients. This then allows other species to colonise the area as its hostility is reduced. These new species are now better adapted to the environment and so compete with pioneer species for light and nutrients. Since they are better adapted, they will out-compete the pioneer species and thus increase their population size. This process of interspecific competition is repeated until a dynamic equilibrium of species is achieved in a climax community. Therefore, there is a continuous interaction between all the organisms, as above, and animals that are maybe involved in seed dispersal or increasing the quality of any soil.

Another interaction between a human and bacteria is that of a human using bacteria for gene therapy. For example, humans use bacteria to produce the hormone insulin for people suffering from type I diabetes. This is achieved by humans using restriction endonucleases which are derived from bacteria to splice a functioning insulin gene out of the DNA. The gene is then inserted into a plasmid by using the same restriction endonucleases and anneals due to the resulting complementary sticky ends. DNA ligases are then used to join the sugar-phosphate backbone on the plasmid. The plasmids are then transferred into a bacterium by placing them in an ice-cold solution of $CaCl_2$ for 15 minutes and then giving them an electric heat shock. The transformed bacteria are then identified by using replica plating and through the help of a marker genes. The transformed bacteria are then grown on mass production and the insulin is extracted.

As hopefully can be seen above, there are many different forms of interactions and relationships between organisms. Some are specifically mutualistic, parasitic or simply part of a cycle. However, without them, it would not be possible for any organism to survive.

A far broader title that brings all of the above together was:

<u>Transfers through ecosystems</u>

Just by seeing this title, I am sure you can appreciate the range of topics that could be incorporated into this. Remembering that you only need to include 4 of those listed below to get full marks for breadth there is no reason why this title could not yield an excellent mark. However, make sure that any paragraph is linked back to what is being TRANSFERRED as the mark scheme below makes clear. Any essay, no matter how complex, that just recites 'everything I know about photosynthesis' will be marked down.

1) Photosynthesis – energy transfer
2) Respiration – energy transfer
3) Carbon cycle (no longer specifically in the specification)
4) Nitrogen cycle
5) Phosphate cycle
6) Food chains
7) Ecological pyramids
8) Pesticide toxicity/bioaccumulation
9) Eutrophication
10) Digestion and absorption
11) Transfer of genetic material
12) Water cycle

Without the transfer of energy and molecules through ecosystems, life would not be able to survive on the planet. At the start of all phototrophic food chains is light energy, or heat in the case of thermotrophs on the seabed, which it transfers into chemical energy. This is then transferred amongst organisms till they die, where it is then transferred back to the environment in a range of forms. In the essay below, I will summarise these transfers and a number of other relevant examples.

As mentioned above, a major transfer is that of light energy into chemical energy during photosynthesis. The transfer into glucose is not a direct one, but rather by a series of steps in the light dependent and then independent reactions. The energy in the photons of light at 680nm hits the chlorophyll molecule of photosystem and excites two electrons from magnesium to the state where the atom is ionised. As the electrons are now free from their shells due to their higher energy, they can move down a series of transmembrane proteins called the electron transport chain. As the electron move along these transfer their energy, and it is used to move protons from the stroma to the inside of the grana/lamellae by active transport. This formed gradient is a store of energy that can be released by the protons facilitated diffusion through ATP synthetase that is also in the membrane. This movement, or kinetic energy, is transferred into chemical energy by the synthesis of ATP from ADP and P_i. In a similar way, the reducing agent NADPH is formed. As can be seen, the light energy is transferred through a number steps to chemical energy in ATP which, in turn, is converted to glucose in the light independent reactions/Calvin cycle.

This molecule of glucose is converted into other molecules within the plant. These are then ingested by a consumer or decomposer if it has died and this chemical energy is then transferred to another trophic level within the ecosystem. Within this organism, the chemical energy can be converted into other forms by respiration. A good example would be movement and muscle contraction. In respiration, the glucose is converted back to carbon dioxide, so the carbon molecule moves back into the atmosphere, as does the water. The energy released goes through the intermediate of ATP and then can be made into movement and heat energy.

As well as these examples, which include carbon, there is also the movement of nitrogen. Nitrogen exists as a gas in the atmosphere. Nitrogen fixing bacteria are able to transfer this to a soluble solid from in nitrates, which can then be transferred into plants and their proteins/DNA. As before, this can be transferred along food chains by consumers until in the end saprophytes and detritivores cause the nitrates to go back into the soil in the form of ammonia. This can be transferred back into nitrates by the further action of bacteria. Some of this nitrogen is then transferred back into the atmosphere by denitrifying bacteria as they remove the oxygen from the molecule in anaerobic conditions to be able to survive. Strangely, about 1% of nitrate formation is by thunder strikes, which provide enough energy for the formation of nitrates from atmospheric nitrogen and oxygen directly.

Due to the use of fertilisers, humans sometimes cause the unintentional transfer of nitrates. If this is not controlled, it can lead on to eutrophication. Here nitrates are washed from the land due to their solubility, and when in still water they can cause an algal bloom. Due to this transfer of nitrates into the algae, they grow and block out the light to plants underneath. These die and are broken down by decomposers. This increase in biological oxygen demand is due to their respiration, coupled to reduced photosynthesis, which means the concentration of oxygen in the water decreases, and there is less life in the water. Another negative example of transfers would be the bioaccumulation of toxins. The most well-known example is the pesticide DDT. This is lipid soluble so is bound to the adipose tissue of organisms and goes up the food chain. As it does so, the concentrations increase to the top predators. In the case of birds of prey, it caused their shells to become so thin the offspring were not born.

Another inorganic ion that is transferred is phosphate. Unlike carbon and nitrogen, it does not enter a gas phase but instead is always a solid. For vast periods of time it is part of a compound in rocks and by weathering becomes soluble it can be absorbed by plants and then passes through the food chains. It can find itself transferred to the bottom of the oceans as organisms die and is therefore incorporated into rocks again by sedimentation.

As can be seen above, many molecules are transferred through ecosystems and without this continuous 'churn' life would stop existing and evolving.

The cycle that has been most commonly referred to is the carbon cycle and is the stem of these essays. However, the carbon cycle is no longer in the AQA spec at A-level. Once I remove this content from these essays they look far more spartan. However, I have included them for completeness and there are aspects that may be of use to you.

Carbon dioxide may affect organisms directly or indirectly. Describe and explain these effects

Carbon dioxide is a greenhouse gas that directly affects the growth of plants and the distribution of insects, but also indirectly influences the activity of organisms and could even lead to speciation of new organisms.

Carbon dioxide levels affect the rate of plant growth, as CO_2 is an essential part of the light independent stages of photosynthesis. The CO_2 is fixated with a molecule of ribulose bisphosphate by the rubisco enzyme to create an unstable 6-carbon compound. This dissipates to form 2 more stable molecules of glycerate-3-phosphate. This then undergoes reduction by NADPH and phosphorylation by ATP to form 2 molecules of triose phosphates. Some of the triose phosphates are assimilated to make glucose and the rest is regenerated by another molecule of ATP to reform ribulose bisphosphate. As CO_2 is usually a limiting factor, increasing the CO_2 concentration, which usually increases productivity in terms of percentage yield of plants/crops.

Fluctuating CO_2 concentrations have an indirect impact on the speciation of fish. This is because CO_2

concentrations of the atmosphere increase, thus causing an equilibrium shift of CO_2 (g) + H_2O (l)$\longleftrightarrow$ H_2CO_3 and thereby decreasing the pH of the water. This change in selection pressures would provide a selective advantage to fish with alleles that favour the acidic conditions, as they are more likely to survive and thus more probable to pass on their advantageous allele to the next generation, thus causing a change in the allele frequency. This, over time, would lead to variation and eventually speciation.

Carbon dioxide also plays a huge role in the internal functioning of the human body with particular reference to the transport of oxygen. Oxygen is transported around the body in the blood, where it is bound to haemoglobin forming oxyhaemoglobin. As haemoglobin is a protein molecule and proteins are affected by pH changes; as the partial pressures of CO_2 change, so does the shape of the haemoglobin. This affects the affinity of the haemoglobin to the oxygen. This is advantageous as it means that muscle, where there is a high rate of aerobic respiration, has a greater demand for oxygen and a high production of CO_2. These high partial pressures of CO_2 lower the affinity of the haemoglobin to oxygen, thus satisfying the oxygen demand by muscle cells, where it can be used as a terminal e-acceptor. This is known as the Bohr Effect.

Carbon dioxide levels in the blood also have a direct impact on the heart rate in mammals. If the CO_2 levels in the blood increases, it causes the pH of the blood to decrease. This change in pH is detected by specialised chemoreceptors found in the carotid artery. They convert this chemical stimulus into electrical impulses that are sent to the medulla oblongata via nerve fibres. The medulla oblongata communicates this information and sends impulses along sympathetic nervous fibres to the S.A.N, causing an increase in heart rate and thus the increased removal of CO_2. This, therefore, returns the pH levels back to a natural homeostatic level, thus completing the negative feedback loop.

Carbon dioxide levels also indirectly affect the distributions of ectotherms, such as lizards. As atmospheric CO_2 levels rise, so do the global temperatures, because CO_2 is a greenhouse gas that traps IR radiation reflected from the earth and re-radiates it back towards the ground, thereby increasing the temperature. And as ectotherms cannot maintain their body temperature internally, external changes to temperature affect the behavioural pattern and habitat locations. They will tend to migrate to temperatures that are more favourable.

The activity of detritivores and saprobionts are also indirectly affected by CO_2 concentrations. As described previously, the increasing CO_2 levels result in increased plant growth. This eventually means increased plant death which means that organic matter is not a limiting factor for detritivores and saprobionts. The detritivores break down the dead organic matter to increase the surface area via holozoic nutrition. The saprobionts then digest the organic matter through the release of extra-cellular enzymes. They then absorb the products of digestion and respire aerobically.

So, as can be seen above, changing carbon dioxide concentrations can have an affect both inside an organism and also in greater ecosystems. As a result, it is an essential molecule in every way, from photosynthesis and the production of glucose to its role of metabolism and blood.

Two other titles have referenced the Carbon Cycle and I have included their mark schemes below. By now I'm sure that you could construct your own essay based on those above:

The transfer of substances containing carbon between organisms and between organisms and the environment

1) Food chains and feeding relationships:
plant producers; idea of food chains as feeding relationships; with transfer energy; in substances containing carbon.
2) Digestion and absorption (possible link to bacteria and fungi):
digestion/hydrolysis of large carbon-containing compounds; by enzymes; producing small/soluble compounds, which can be absorbed.
3) Transport of organic molecules in and out of cells/across exchange surface (possible link to bacteria and fungi):
organic molecules (including sugars and amino acids) cross cell membranes; by facilitated diffusion; active transport; which requires ATP from respiration; involving carrier proteins and/or enzymes.
4) Photosynthesis:

light-independent reaction; carbon dioxide reacts with ribulose bisphosphate; glycerate 3-P reduced to sugar; reduced NADP and ATP from light-dependent reaction; Calvin cycle.
5) Respiration:
link reaction/Krebs cycle; oxidation of intermediates; generation of reduced coenzymes; loss of carbon dioxide.
6) Exchange surfaces – for carbon dioxide for animals and plants;
large surface area – alveoli – mesophyll cells; short diffusion pathways – epithelium and endothelium – thin leaves and many stomata; maintaining diffusion gradient – capillary and respiration – photosynthesis; respiration in mesophyll cells (time of day); ventilation – breathing – via air spaces in leaf.

Carbon dioxide in organisms and ecosystems

1) The biochemistry of photosynthesis
2) The biochemistry of respiration
3) Gas exchange surfaces
4) Changes in cardiac output and pulmonary ventilation with exercise
5) The transport of respiratory gases
6) The effect of carbon dioxide on productivity;
7) Decomposition and recycling maintain the balance of nutrients in an ecosystem
8) The greenhouse effect is not specifically mentioned but should be credited here, if discussed

Other...

The final set of essays have alternative stems, but by now I hope that you can see that the content is all very similar to what that has gone before, but in a different sequence. There have been surprisingly few with a general 'physiological' title, and the only one that I could really find is this one and candidates tended to avoid the essay as they think they don't know anything about it. One of the few cycles is below.

Negative feedback in living organisms

However, if we look at the possible elements that could be included below you will see the range that is possible. As with many of these things, it is important to make sure that all of your comments answer the question specifically. So, rather than write everything that you know about homeostasis, make sure that you specifically relate it to the role of negative feedback. As always, you would not be expected to include all of them and the following essay is of an A* standard.

1) The principle of negative feedback – departure from a norm initiates changes which restore a system to the norm.
2) The importance in homeostasis; principles of detection of change, the role of receptors, corrective response, the role of effectors.
3) Thermoregulation; the roles of thermoreceptors and hypothalamus in detection; heat loss and heat gain centres; sweating and vasodilatation in heat loss; vasoconstriction, hair erection, shivering and increased metabolism in heat gain.

4) The regulation of blood glucose; the roles of receptors in pancreas, secretion of insulin or glucagon; effect of insulin on surface membrane receptors/carrier proteins in stimulating uptake of glucose and glycogenesis; the role of glucagon in glycogenolysis.

5) The control of ventilation; stimulation of chemoreceptors in medulla; effect on inspiration; stimulation of stretch receptors in lungs; stimulation of expiratory cells in medulla.

6)The control of heartbeat; roles of chemoreceptors and pressure receptors; inhibitory and acceleratory centres in medulla; effect on SAN and the rate of heartbeat; effect of change in rate on pH/pressure of blood.

7) The metabolic pathways; examples of the build-up of a product in a metabolic pathway resulting in inhibition of its formation – enzyme inhibition.

8) Population stability; effect of increasing competition/predation on increasing population size and restoration of balance.

9) Selection, stabilising selection, resulting in the constancy of species.

Negative feedback is a crucial principle in living organisms, as it allows the maintenance of constant conditions where an extreme, either side, would damage the organism. Negative feedback mechanisms work through the idea that a departure from the fixed normal state of a system triggers changes which will return that system to the norm. This is involved primarily in homeostasis, the maintenance of a constant internal environment, with these individual changes being detected by receptors and then corrected by effectors.

One homeostatic system is that of thermoregulation, the maintenance of a constant internal temperature, which is necessary for enzyme action, as enzymes have an optimal temperature for catalysing reactions – roughly 37°C in humans. Thermoreceptors in the hypothalamus monitor internal temperature by detecting changes in the blood temperature, and thermoreceptors on the skin monitor external temperature. When thermoreceptors detect that the temperature is too high, the hypothalamus sends signals to effectors that in endotherms trigger various mechanisms to decrease temperature. For example, sweating increases, with the sweat taking away heat as it evaporates, and arterioles near the surface of the skin dilate in vasodilation directing blood to capillary networks closer to the skin as heat is lost through radiation. This leads to a greater loss of heat, returning the temperature to the optimal level in a negative feedback process. Similarly, if the temperature is too low, then sweating decreases and blood is directed away from capillary networks close to the surface, in vasoconstriction. The hair on the surface is made to stand up by the contraction of erector pili muscles, which provides an insulating layer of air trapped in the hair. In addition, the body produces hormones, such as adrenaline, that increase the metabolism and thus generate more heat, and muscles contract in shivering, producing yet more heat, all done to return the temperature to the norm.

Another homeostatic system that relies on negative feedback is that of the control of blood glucose. Here, receptors in the pancreas detect when the blood glucose level goes below or above the correct amount, and cells in the pancreas are stimulated to release a relevant hormone, glucagon from α-cells, if blood glucose is too low, and insulin from β-cells, if it is too high. Glucagon stimulates glycogenolysis, in which glycogen stored in cells is broken down to make glucose, and gluconeogenesis, in which new glucose is made from other substances and stimulates cells to release glucose into the blood, and so increases blood glucose concentration back to the normal. Insulin stimulates cells to take up glucose from the blood and undergo glycogenesis, in which excess glucose is stored as glycogen and so decreases blood glucose levels down to the normal level again. These are, therefore, both negative feedback mechanisms.

Negative feedback is also involved in the menstrual cycle. An increase in FSH concentration, for example, stimulates the ovary to release oestrogen, which then inhibits the production of FSH, keeping it at a low level – this ensures that only one follicle develops in the early stages of the cycle. Later, an increase in LH stimulates the development of the corpus luteum, which then produces progesterone. This progesterone then inhibits further release of LH in another negative feedback loop that, again, prevents additional follicles forming.

The control of ventilation and heartbeat also works through a negative feedback mechanism. Chemoreceptors in the medulla detect when the blood's acidity changes, with an increase meaning that the blood's carbon dioxide concentration has increased and its oxygen concentration has, therefore, decreased. As oxygen is necessary as the terminal electron acceptor in respiration, and an overly high level of carbon dioxide can be harmful, the acceleratory centre in the medulla stimulates the SAN to make the heart beat stronger and more frequently. This is so that blood can be pumped to the lungs, to be reoxygenated and have its carbon dioxide removed, and so act in a negative feedback loop to make the acidity decrease. Conversely, a decrease in acidity results in the inhibitory centre, slowing and decreasing the strength at which the heart beats. Baroreceptors in the heart can stimulate a similar effect, with an increase in blood pressure resulting in the heartbeat being slowed down, so that blood pressure decreases, and vice versa, so that blood pressure is controlled at a fixed level.

Finally, negative feedback can also be seen outside the body in an ecological perspective, as populations tend to remain roughly stable. When intraspecific competition is low, for example, a population's size tends to increase, as there is an excess of resources. However, once the population increases too much, competition increases and resources are comparatively scarce, meaning that the population decreases. The size, therefore, oscillates around a certain level, with an increase above this leading to a negative feedback loop causing it to decrease, and vice versa. Predation has a similar effect – when other factors are removed, an increase in a predator's population size will cause a decrease in its prey's, which will then, after a lag, cause a decrease in the predator's population, as it's food source becomes scarcer. This, therefore, increases the size of the prey's population, increasing the predator's again, as its food source is more abundant. These negative feedback loops again keep population sizes stable and restore the balance, which is their function throughout biology.

As can hopefully be seen from the examples above, negative feedback can function on a cellular, organism and ecosystem level. The evolution of these systems must have been complex, but the ability of any organism to maintain and control its environment is essential for its survival and subsequent reproductive success.

To try and make this book complete, I have also looked at essay titles that AQA has published in advisory publications to schools. These have not been set as real exam questions and therefore do not have an *official* mark scheme I can refer to. Below is an example of such a title. The author, a solid A* candidate, has written a piece based on what we thought the mark scheme might be. The fact this sort of title has never been asked might reflect how likely it is to be asked in your exam!

Ways in which different species of organisms differ from each other

1) Genetics

2) Cellular   Plant cells vs Animal Cells

Eukaryotic cells vs Prokaryotic cells

3) Coordination

Nervous systems

Hormonal systems/plant growth factors

Gas exchange mechanisms

On the planet, there are over 8.7 million different species and since the beginning of life on Earth, this accounts for less than 1% of the species that have existed. These species are very different from one another and there are many explanations for these differences: very different genetic makeups, different environments, molecular differences etc. This essay will explore some of the main differences between organisms and the reasons for these differences.

The most profound difference between organisms is between prokaryotes and eukaryotes. Prokaryotes are single-celled organisms, which do not contain any membrane bound organelles (bacteria), and eukaryotes, which describe the other four kingdoms that living things are classified into (animals, plants, fungi and protoctists.) Prokaryotes do contain ribosomes but they are smaller in size compared to the ribosomes, which are present in eukaryotic cells. There are many differences between prokaryotic and eukaryotic cells, but one of the main ones is how the DNA is arranged. In prokaryotes, there is a loop of DNA that exists freely in the cytoplasm, whereas in eukaryotes, the DNA is associated with proteins (histones) and exists as chromatin during most of the interphase in the cell cycle, and as chromosomes during mitosis. Furthermore, prokaryotic organisms often contain small sections of DNA which carry survival value, as plasmids. These code for proteins that can aid the cell's survival; for example, many plasmids contain genes for antibiotic resistance. Not only can plasmids be passed on to daughter cells when the bacterium divides (vertical gene transmission) but they can also be passed directly on to other bacteria, even of a different species (horizontal gene transmission.) During this process, the plasmid is replicated and passed from one bacterium to another, along a conjugation tube.

As previously mentioned, prokaryotes lack membrane bound organelles, which means they have no mitochondria. Eukaryotes are able to respire aerobically, due to the presence of the mitochondria. When glucose has been phosphorylated and splits into 2 molecules of glycerate-3-phosphate, it is then oxidised by the coenzyme NAD to form pyruvate. 2 molecules (net) of ATP are produced by substrate-level phosphorylation. Pyruvate then enters the mitochondria through its double membrane and undergoes the link reaction, when it is further oxidised by another NAD molecule and decarboxylated. It then joins with coenzyme A to form acetyl coenzyme A. This then enters the Krebs cycle. The acetyl coenzyme A joins with oxaloacetate and citrate is produced. Citrate then undergoes a series of redox reactions, as well as 2 stages of decarboxylation. The result of this is that several coenzymes (NAD and FAD) are produced, as well as 2 molecules of carbon dioxide, and oxaloacetate is regenerated. Some ATP is produced, again by substrate level phosphorylation. The link reaction and Krebs cycle both occur in the matrix of the mitochondria. In the final stage of respiration, the reduced coenzymes are oxidised at protein pumps, which are embedded in the inner membrane of the mitochondria. The electrons released enter an electron transport chain, where they undergo a series of redox reactions. They travel from a high energy state to a low energy state and this energy is used to pump protons across the inner membrane into the inter membrane space. This creates an electrochemical gradient which the protons diffuse down, though ATP synthase, by chemiosmosis. This energy is used to bring together ATP and Pi to form ATP. The electrons combine with the protons and an oxygen molecule to produce water – hence, the final stage is called oxidative phosphorylation. In prokaryotes however, the only way that ATP is generated is by substrate level phosphorylation during glycolysis. The pyruvate that is produced is reduced by the reduced coenzymes, to produce ethanol. In this way, the coenzymes can be reused. Sometimes, eukaryotes respire anaerobically, but prokaryotes rely solely on this form of respiration in order to generate ATP.

Many of the differences between organisms of different species are due to the fact that they have different genomes. Genes are sections of DNA and the sequence of bases (i.e. the sequence of codons) in the DNA will determine the sequence of amino acids in a protein's primary structure. In this way, DNA controls the shape and function of the protein which the cell produces. If, however, the proteins produced are significantly different, due to differences in DNA, it will affect the appearance and functions of the organism. The processes by which DNA is used to produce proteins are called transcription and translation. Firstly, the DNA is used as a template to produce a molecule of pre-mRNA, using RNA polymerase. This is then spliced to remove the non-coding sections called introns. The mRNA then leaves the nucleus through a nuclear pore and travels through the cytoplasm so that it can join with a ribosome. The ribosome translates the mRNA by 'reading' each codon and the tRNA with the complementary anticodon brings the correct amino acid to the ribosome. In this way, the sequence of amino acids is built up and they can form peptide bonds. Once the polypeptide is completed, it is transported to the Golgi apparatus where it will fold up into specific 3D shape and can be stored in a vesicle. One protein which is present in animals, but differs greatly from species to species is haemoglobin. The function of haemoglobin is to transport oxygen around the body. The affinity for oxygen, however, can change and animals that live in regions with a lower partial pressure of oxygen (e.g. at high altitudes) will have haemoglobin molecules with a higher affinity for oxygen. This means that oxygen will associate to the haem group(s) at a lower partial pressure. This is advantageous because the animal lives in a region with a low partial pressure of oxygen, so if the haemoglobin had a lower affinity for oxygen, it is likely that not enough oxygen would associate to the haemoglobin. This is but one example, and many differences in the proteins produced can cause differences in the appearance of organisms. For example, if the protein in question is an enzyme that leads to pigmentation, different forms of the enzyme could affect the pigments and cause differences in the colours produced.

Ultimately, it is the variation in organisms which can cause new or different species to arise. The first stage of this process (speciation) is geographical or reproductive isolation. In allopatric speciation, the barrier can often be something along the lines of a river or mountain range. In sympatric speciation, there is usually a type of reproductive isolation, caused by differences in courtship or other aspects of behaviour. In either case, the result is the same: there are 2 different populations of a species, each with its own gene pool and no interbreeding. Obviously, within each population, there is genetic diversity. Also, due to the fact that they may live in different environments, the selection pressures for each population may be different. As a result, organisms with different alleles will have different reproductive success, and those with the alleles which are deemed 'advantageous' with respect to the selection pressure are the most likely to survive. Over time, the allele frequencies change and 2 different species will be eventually formed – in other words, the populations will no longer be able to breed.

In conclusion, organisms differ from each other, not only due to differences in their genotypes, but also due to behavioural traits. It is also important to note that even if organisms have the same genotype for a gene, they may not appear the same because the phenotype is the result of both the genotype and the environment. This explains why even organisms with identical genes (i.e. twins) can often have different appearances.

Reflecting on this idea of differences, a previous title of the essay was:

<u>Apart from causing disease, describe how bacteria may affect the lives of other organisms</u>

1) Commercial production of enzymes from microorganisms
2) Gene technology
3) Bacteria's role in the recycling of nutrients in the nitrogen cycle
4) Cellulose digestion in ruminants

Bacteria can affect the lives of humans in both a positive and negative light. Some bacteria are pathogenic and cause disease in humans, whereas others can be used in gene technology to produce various hormones and proteins to treat diseases. Bacteria are also an essential part of the eco-system involved in the recycling of both carbon and nitrogen compounds in the eco-system.

Humans use bacteria in gene technology for the production of insulin. The human insulin gene is isolated using restriction endonucleases that cut the DNA strand at specific recognition sequences. They leave sticky ends, which are small tails of unpaired bases where they cut the DNA. The same restriction enzymes are used to splice a bacterial plasmid. DNA ligases are then used to join the sugar-phosphate backbone between the gene and the bacterial plasmid. The plasmid containing the recombinant DNA of the human insulin gene is transferred into a bacterium by placing it in an ice-cold isotonic solution of Calcium Chloride to increase the permeability of the cell wall. The solution is then given a heat shock to encourage the uptake of the plasmid into the bacterium. The transformed bacteria are then identified by using genetic markers in a process called replica plating. The transformed bacteria are grown in mass culture and the insulin is extracted.

Saprobionts are a type of bacteria that form a vital component of the nitrogen and carbon cycle. The saprobionts release extra-cellular enzymes that digest the protein containing nitrogen via hydrolysis into amino acids and are the deaminated into ammonium ions. Nitrifying bacteria, such as nitrozomas, oxidise the ammonium ions into nitrites and nitrobacta, then oxidise these into nitrates. The nitrates are then actively transported into the root hair cell of plants to be used for the production of amino acids, DNA and RNA, thus completing the nitrogen cycle. Also, the saprobionts themselves absorb the glucose the primary product of digestion and use it as a respiratory substrate. They release the CO_2 into the air for absorption by plants; thus completing the carbon cycle.

The symbiotic relationship of the rhizobium bacteria and leguminous plants are another example of the importance of bacteria. This is a mutualistic relationship where the bacteria are found in the root nodules and work under anaerobic conditions. They convert nitrogen gas found in the air into ammonium ions for the plant. The ammonium ions are a source of nitrogen, which can then be used to make DNA, proteins and RNA. In return, the rhizobium bacteria receive glucose as a product of photosynthesis and use it as the respiratory substrate for respiration. This mutualistic symbiotic relationship helps to complement the survival of both organisms.

Some bacteria are commensal organisms that in fact protect human from disease and the invasion of pathogenic bacteria. They form part of the first line of defence. They live on the surface of the skin and out-compete pathogenic bacteria for the nutrients and minerals needed for survival. This form of interspecific competition reduces the population size of the pathogenic bacteria on the skin and thus reduces the likelihood of a disease forming on cut skin. In a similar way, bacteria that are able to digest cellulose that live in the intestine of ruminant animals. These release extra-cellular cellulose that digests cellulose to the constituent β-glucose molecules. These can be absorbed by the ruminants, such as cows, and the bacteria get access to amino acids, as well as a good habitat.

As can be seen above, the relationship between bacteria and higher living organisms can be positive and I hope I have described a range of ways in which this is the case.

The Cause of Disease in Humans

There has been quite a bit of change here with the removal of any content on microorganisms as pathogens and diseases of the heart and lungs. Diabetes has been added and there are no named examples in terms of genetics, as there used to be. To this end, I have removed the mark scheme and included some relevant paragraphs from two candidates' essays. However, I do not see how this can form an essay next year.

The other major cause of diseases in humans is genetic diseases. These arise as a result of random mutation, which often occurs in the S phase of interphase during cell division. This can cause an alteration in the DNA base sequence of an exon region, which can then result in a production of a malfunctioning protein due to a different amino acid sequence. For example, a mutation in the Brca gene, which is a class of tumour suppressor genes, could result in cancer. The Brca 1 gene codes for a transcription factor that binds to operon region of genes involved in cell division and suppresses cell division. However, if mutated, a transcription factor with a different shape would be produced and so would no longer be able to bind to these regions on the DNA and so no longer suppress cell division. The Brca 2 gene is also involved in DNA repair mechanisms, and if this mutates it will result in an inability to repair any mutations that occur.

Diabetes is a condition caused when blood glucose concentration is not controlled in the usual manner, by using insulin. There are two types of diabetes, type one and type two. Type one is a disease that you are born with and is due to genetic factors, whereas type two is due to lifestyle factors and can develop later in life. Type two diabetes is often linked to obesity because the beta cells cannot produce enough insulin to cope with the excessive amount of glucose in the blood. It can also be caused when the receptors to insulin on the cell membranes of human cells are not functioning properly due to being previously over-worked. Therefore, the cells do not take up enough glucose, leaving it in the blood, which results in a higher glucose concentration. Controlling the person's diet, so that they aren't taking in too many carbohydrates and are losing weight, can help to treat type two diabetes.

Type one diabetes is a disease caused by genetic factors. It occurs when the beta cells in the islets of Langerhans don't produce any insulin. Thus, when someone with type one diabetes eats something their blood glucose level rises and doesn't fall, which causes hyperglycaemia and can result in death if untreated. The kidneys cannot cope with such a high level of glucose, so excrete some of it in urine, a process that can cause kidney failure. Type one diabetes can be treated by injections of insulin, so that the person can convert the glucose. However, this has to be strictly controlled to avoid hypoglycaemia, which occurs when glucose levels in the blood are too low.

Genetics and DNA

Surprisingly, only a handful of essays have had a stem that is directly linked to genetics. I have put them together in the last 40 titles. Whether this is a particular topic that you directly prepare for, I will leave up to you.

Why the offspring produced by the same parents are different in appearance

1) Genes incorporate coded information which influences phenotype
2) Gene mutation
3) Environment variation
4) Dietary requirements of insects
5) Meiosis
6) Principles of Mendelian inheritance
7) Polygenetic inheritance
8) Gametes and gamete formation, fertilisation

Despite being produced from the same parents, offspring still appear different. This is due to variation among both their genotypes and the environments they have developed in, for both of these contribute to the phenotype. In the former, variation created through sexual reproduction means that different versions of a protein are produced, and in the latter, variation causes genes to be expressed differently, as well as having more direct effects.

The reason that differences in genetics cause differences in appearance is that these genetics incorporate coded information, with each gene coding for the production of a particular protein. mRNA is transcribed from the gene in the nucleus, with RNA polymerase attaching before the gene, unzipping it, and binding complementary RNA nucleotides together. After non-coding intron sections are spliced out in eukaryotic cells, the mRNA leaves the nucleus and travels to ribosomes, such as those embedded in the skin of the rough endoplasmic reticulum. Moving from the start codon, a complementary anticodon on tRNA attaches to each codon on the mRNA, and as each tRNA molecule has an amino acid attached, these are all attached together with peptide bonds by the ribosome, which requires ATP, to make a protein. These proteins affect the structure and function of different cells, and therefore of the body as a whole. In fact, it is the genes that are expressed in cells – initially based on local conditions – that cause them to become specialised by creating permanent conditions, which express the specific genes for the function of that cell. If proteins differ, such as through a recessive version of a gene that produces a non-functioning version of a protein, then the appearance of an individual will be different. Mutations – mistakes made in copying the genetic information – cause these differences, leading to different amino acids being used to make the protein, due to different triplets existing in the DNA. If the mutation is a substitution, it can be silent, leading to no change in the protein. This is due to the degenerate nature of the DNA code, with multiple different triplet codes coding for the same amino acid. But if it is a deletion, then the protein will change, as it creates a frame shift, changing the position of all subsequent triplets.

Offspring of the same parents are genetically different due to the process of meiosis, which creates gametes that only contain one set of genetic information, unlike the two that feature in normal cells. Two gametes, one from each parent, combine in fertilisation, and so the child inherits half of each parent's genetic information. Homologous chromosomes are separated in the first division, meiosis I. These chromosomes are then split, as would occur in mitosis, in meiosis II, creating cells with only one allele of each gene. Which of the two different chromosomes go into each cell is random, so there are many possible combinations of different chromosomes in the gametes, creating variation among the offspring. In addition, before meiosis I, homologous chromosomes can exchange some of their genetic material by forming a chiasma, in a process called chromosomal crossover, which creates even more variation among what genetic information can be included in gametes. According to the principles of Mendelian inheritance, each of the offspring inherits one copy of each gene from each parent, due to the combination of gametes in fertilisation, each of which consists of one set of genetic information. These alleles can be either dominant or recessive, with dominant expressing the characteristic it codes for, even if only one copy is present, and recessive only doing so if both alleles are recessive. If, for example, one of two offspring inherits a dominant from one parent and a recessive from the other, and the other inherits recessives from both parents, the first will show the dominant characteristic and the second the recessive. Although genetics is far more complicated than this, with multiple genes actually coding for most characteristics, this principle applies regardless.

Variation in the environment can also cause the offspring of the same parents to appear different. Although an organism may have alleles that would make it taller than average; for example, if it is undernourished or develops in an environment with restricted space, this characteristic would not be fully expressed. This is what causes identical twins who have identical genotypes, as they are made by the division of a single zygote, to still appear slightly different. Their fingerprints, for example, are distinguishable due to small variations in the part of the womb they gestated in. In addition, gene expression within cells is controlled by transcription factors, which bind to a promoter region on the template DNA, either making it easier for RNA polymerase to attach and therefore acting to stimulate expression of that gene, or preventing RNA polymerase from attaching and therefore acting to block expression. The hormone oestrogen, for example, can act as either type of transcription factor, by binding to an oestrogen receptor in the cytoplasm to make an oestrogen-oestrogen receptor complex – whether this blocks or stimulates transcription depends on the type of cell and the specific gene. As the level of oestrogen can be determined partially by the environment, this can affect whether a gene is expressed, and therefore alter the genotype.

As can be seen above, there are a number of causes, both genetic and environmental that can cause a difference in the phenotype of the offspring. This variation is essential, so that evolution can occur and a species can adapt to changes in the environment. Often mate selection in higher animals is based on the perceived strength of a potential partner's phenotype. This means that as the generations progress, so the differences between each generation get bigger and more polarised.

An entirely different title was asked one year. I have included this below.

Use of DNA in Science and Technology

1) *DNA and classification*
2) *Structure of DNA*
3) *Differences in DNA lead to genetic diversity*
4) *Comparison of DNA base sequences*
5) *DNA hybridisation*
6) *Genetic engineering and making useful substances*
7) *Plasmids*
8) *The use of recombinant DNA to produce transformed organisms that benefit humans*
9) *Cell cycle and treatment of cancer*
10) *Gene therapy;*
11) *Medical diagnosis and the treatment of human disease;*
12) *The use of DNA probes to screen patients for clinically important genes*

DNA stands for deoxyribonucleic acid and is composed of a phosphate group, a deoxyribose pentose sugar and a nitrogenous base, either adenine, guanine, thymine or cytosine. It is a double helix made up of two strands. In one strand, the nucleic acids are bonded together by phosphodiester bonds forming a sugar phosphate backbone. The two strands run anti-parallel and are held together by hydrogen bonds between the complementary base pairs. The DNA contains exons (coding regions) and introns (non-coding regions). The coding regions have specific base sequences that are transcribed into pre-mRNA, which then go on to be translated by the ribosome into proteins. As we understand, parts of the introns serve no function, but much of it is involved in acting as promoter region sequences for genes.

Gene Therapy is a dynamic area of medical research. It uses DNA technology to treat various genetic disorders, such as SCID* (Severe combined immunodeficiency syndrome), where sufferers have a mutation in the ADA gene and thus produce a malfunctioning adenosine deaminase enzyme, which makes the T lymphocytes susceptible to being destroyed by toxins from invading pathogens. For treatment, a functioning ADA gene can be isolated from the DNA of a healthy patient by using various restriction endonucleases. This isolated gene can then be spliced into the DNA of a DNA virus using DNA ligases to join the sugar phosphate backbone. The virus is then used as a vector to transfer the functioning ADA gene into pluripotent stem cells extracted from the bone marrow of a sufferer. The transformed bone marrow cells are then placed back into the patient. These now divide and differentiate into fully function T lymphocytes, as they have a functioning ADA gene producing the functioning adenosine deaminase enzyme breaking down toxins that infect the T lymphocyte.

DNA technology is also used in the pharmaceutical industry for the production of human insulin. mRNA coding for the human insulin protein is extracted from the beta cells in the islets of Langerhans. The isolated mRNA is incubated with reverse transcriptase and free-floating DNA nucleotides. The single stranded cDNA is converted to double stranded cDNA using DNA polymerase and DNA nucleotides. The cDNA now coding for the human insulin protein is spliced into a bacterial plasmid. The plasmid is then transferred into a bacterium by placing it in an ice-cold isotonic solution of calcium chloride to increase the permeability of the cell wall. The solution is then given a heat shock to encourage the uptake of the plasmid into the bacterium. The transformed bacteria are identified by using genetic markers in a process called replica plating. The transformed bacteria are grown in mass culture and the insulin is extracted.

DNA technology is also used by evolutionary biologists to investigate the genetic relationships between different organisms in a process called DNA hybridisation. DNA samples from two different organisms are compared by first radioactively labelling one of the samples. The DNA samples from both organisms are then mixed and incubated to a temperature of around 95^C, so that the hydrogen bonds between the DNA samples are broken. It is then cooled to room temperature, allowing some DNA from organism one to anneal to some of the DNA from organism 2. The mixture is then heated at regular intervals and followed, using UV light to see at what temperature the DNA strands separate. The higher the temperature, the more hydrogen bonds are present between the DNA strands, and the more similar the base sequences between the two samples are, and so the more closely related the organisms are.

Forensic science uses DNA technology in the form of PCR to amplify a sample of DNA found at a crime scene so it can be analysed via genetic fingerprinting. The DNA sample is amplified by incubating it in a thermocycler with activated DNA nucleotides, primers and a thermally stable *Taq* polymerase. The amplified sample can then be mixed with specific restriction endonucleases, which cut up the DNA fragments at specific recognition sequences. The samples of DNA fragments are then placed into a well on an agar gel that is immersed in a dilute aqueous alkali solution. Electrodes are placed on either side and a current applied that separates the DNA fragments, according to their varying lengths. The patterns are analysed by fixing the fragments onto a nylon adsorbent membrane, using filter paper for a capillary action and UV light. Radioactively labelled DNA probes that are complementary to mini-satellites on the DNA sample are then washed over the nylon membrane. An X-ray film is then developed to analyse and compare the bands of DNA.

One thing that is certain is that the advances in the use of DNA will continue to increase. Already doctors are using genome screening to target and select specific chemotherapy drugs and screen patients before the symptoms of diseases are detectable. Genetics and genomics has the possibility of being as important as the industrial revolution for mankind.

CONCLUSION

As I've stated all along, there is no need to try and learn these essays. That would be a foolhardy endeavour which would inevitably lead to failure. Instead, I have provided you with a selection of A/A* essay plans for each title there has been over the last 20 years. As I said in the introduction, your best 'tactic' is just to practice and use these essays as a guidance. I also stress that you need to see how useful a number of model paragraphs are, as these can be manipulated to answer the title being asked.

.

Printed in Great Britain
by Amazon

46575962R00084